August 2023

SEA &
SHORE

RECIPES AND STORIES FROM
A KITCHEN IN CORNWALL

EMILY SCOTT

PHOTOGRAPHY BY KIM LIGIITBODY

Hardie Grant

BOOKS

To my children, Oscar, Finn and Evie.
This book is for you.
Mama xx

CONTENTS

7   Introduction

14   Cornwall

26   Early years

28   A cook and her kitchen

30   A sense of place

31   Kitchen notes and essential recipes

56   **WINTER SEAS**

82   **NOËL – SMALL WONDERS**

100   **SPRING TIDES**

144   **SUMMER SEAS**

180   **HIGH SUMMER**

210   **AUTUMN TIDES**

244   Suppliers

246   Emily Scott

250   Index

255   La fin

INTRODUCTION

Cornwall is where I found my home and my heart, my soulmate. It's where my children have been lucky enough to spend carefree days by the sea, messing around on boats in Port Isaac harbour, whiling away the hours fishing for shrimps and crabs in the rock pools, walking down to the wall and looking out towards the ever-changing ocean beyond. Over the years, with parts of my life spent in Provence, Burgundy and Bordeaux, as well as Cornwall, I have developed a passion for simple, seasonal cooking with beautiful ingredients. This cookbook brings together that passion and those worlds, but Cornwall is certainly the cherry on top of the cake, for me. It's where I feel at home and it inspires the food I love to cook and share.

Cornwall is such an inspiring place to be connected to. So close, coast to coast, the wonders of the unashamedly rugged north coast, with surfing bays where the waves bash the beaches and where the weather can change in front of you, contrasts with the softness of the south coast, with sailing boats, palm trees and flourishing flowers. It is a place for all of your senses. Exciting in all seasons, with rich pickings from nature by the seaside.

I am often asked how I cook. I like to use few ingredients and let them shine. Less really is more, on my plate. Cooking, for me, is not always about being the best. It is about having a go, learning something new and being part of something. I love going to my local farmers' market, meandering among the stalls, talking to the producers, smelling, tasting, and planning what I am going to cook. My recipes are mostly simple; the secret to getting them right is a little thought, time and enthusiasm. Be enthusiastic – enthusiasm moves the world.

I hope, with this book, to inspire you to get cooking; to inspire you to shop with your local butcher, fishmonger and grocery store; to get a feel for the seasons and provenance. I would love for you to get excited about the ingredients and to make a list (I am an obsessive list writer, although I'm not sure that always makes me efficient). This is a book that has been on my mind for ten years – it has most definitely been a work in progress, something that I hoped to achieve at some point. Like the sayings 'good things come to those who wait' or 'patience is a virtue' – which are both things I was taught as a child – I now agree that some things really do take time. Time to grow and learn, time to feel confident enough and, more importantly, time to find the right words. So, here I am at my desk, writing, sharing my thoughts, recipes, moments and memories from my life, from my kitchen in Cornwall and beyond.

Look up and connect to the world around you, to the natural ebb and flow of nature. Norah Jones on the radio, hot buttered toast, a mug of tea...

HELLO, HELLO TO YOU. I am so happy to be here with you all. So, to begin, I have baked you a cake – my carrot cake. A favourite in our house and, of course, a classic.

SPICED CARROT CAKE WITH CREAM CHEESE AND BUTTER ICING (AND NOT A RAISIN OR NUT IN SIGHT)

Serves 8

225 ml (8 fl oz/scant 1 cup) sunflower oil,
   plus extra for greasing
225 g (8 oz/1¼ cups) soft light brown sugar
3 eggs
225 g (8 oz/1¾ cups) self-raising flour
1 teaspoon bicarbonate of soda (baking soda)
1½ teaspoons ground ginger
1½ teaspoons mixed spice
1½ teaspoons ground cinnamon
7 carrots, grated (435 g/15 oz in weight)

For the icing (frosting)
175 g (6 oz) unsalted butter, softened
250 g (9 oz/generous 1 cup) cream cheese,
   at room temperature
200 g (7 oz/generous 1½ cups) icing
   (confectioner's) sugar, sifted

To decorate (optional)
edible viola flowers
edible gold leaf or silver glitter

Preheat the oven to 170°C (150°C fan/340°F/Gas 3). Grease and line the base and sides of a round 20 cm (8 in) cake tin (pan) with baking parchment.

In a large bowl, whisk together the oil, sugar and eggs until smooth. Add the flour, bicarbonate of soda and spices to the bowl and mix to combine. Stir in the carrots.

continued...

Scrape the mixture into the prepared pan and level out the top with a palette knife. Bake in the oven for 1 hour 5 minutes–1 hour 15 minutes, or until a skewer inserted into the middle of the cake comes out clean. Leave to cool in the pan for 5 minutes, then remove from the tin and transfer to a wire rack to cool completely.

To make the icing, beat the softened butter in a large bowl until completely smooth, then add the cream cheese and mix to combine. Beat until smooth. Sift over the icing sugar and mix (carefully at first, otherwise there will be clouds of icing sugar) until smooth and fluffy. Taste – it should be sweet and moreish.

Cut the cooled cake in half horizontally, then use half of the icing to sandwich the halves back together. Place the cake on a cake stand or plate and spread the remaining icing over the top of the cake. Decorate with violas or follow Evie's example and have fun with edible gold and silver glitter. Glitter in the kitchen for days...

There is always time for cake. I never need a reason to bake a cake – the beautiful basics of flour, butter, sugar and eggs. The processes of melting, stirring, beating, whisking, folding and icing bring me great happiness. Whether baking an old-fashioned sponge, muffins, banana bread, pastry or meringues, there is the comfort of watching the magic happen, as my family return home and smell wafts of cake coming from the kitchen. It somehow makes the world seem okay and there is nothing more loving than cooking for family or friends.

CORNWALL

Close your eyes, breath it in. Think of a place where the sky meets the sea, where the weather changes from moment to moment, where the coastline is beautifully rugged and hidden coves nestle among dramatic cliff faces and where surf breaks on beautiful sandy shores. A place of sea shanties, finding treasure (sea glass) on the beaches, building sandcastles, combing for shells, the deliciousness of splits at teatime – jam first, topped with cream – and Cornish pasties (which I usually have a hunger for when I am suitably hungover) with a mug of tea.

Think of mystical valleys, where small patches of precious woodland cascade down towards the sea, where I love the intimacy of wandering, looking up, breathing it all in, down shaded pathways and the sense of adventure as you catch glimpses of the glistening turquoise sea through the trees that hug the rocky coves. On summer days, we head down wooded tracks with cool boxes, the children grasping their fishing nets, baskets filled with blankets, flasks and the weekend papers, the children happy with excitement, while our dogs Monty and Inca charge ahead following the scent of the sea. A little piece of heaven. My happiest childhood memories are of doing just this. The joy of a summer picnic in your own special place is something passed down almost entirely unchanged from generation to generation.

Cornwall is the home of Fisherman's Friends, Doc Martin, Poldark, Daphne du Maurier, sticks of rock, clotted-cream fudge, a '99' ice cream and old-fashioned holidays. A place of endless magic. There is always a dose of 'vitamin sea' nearby and all that nature has to offer. Calm, restorative, uplifting and beautiful...
This is Cornwall.

THE INN – ST. TUDY INN, ST. TUDY, CORNWALL

More than six years have passed since I turned up on the doorstep of the St. Tudy Inn. St. Tudy is a beautiful, rural, inland village in North Cornwall. An escape from the crowded coastline, the village was once home to Captain Bligh of Mutiny on the Bounty fame, and has a picturesque church and a wonderful community shop. Situated on the River Camel, six miles from the market town of Wadebridge, a half-hour drive from Rock, Port Isaac and Padstow, and in easy reach of Bodmin Moor, the St. Tudy Inn has best of both worlds – of being inland but still very close to the coast.

I arrived with my three children, Oscar, Finn and Evie, and dogs Monty and Inca. It was midwinter, a few days before Christmas and I was full of excitement and expectation. There was much to do to open before Christmas. How we did it I will never know, but we did. Christmas 2014 was the start of the greatest adventure.

I love simplicity and a pared-back feel. At the Inn, restful shades of Cornforth White and Purbeck Stone set the backdrop to my schemes – I go back to them time and time again, as they have timeless charm. We have open fireplaces, old wooden crates and beer kegs as stools. I keep the flowers simple, cut from the garden, or I should say my mother's garden. Simple glassware, white plates, and linen dish-towel napkins complete my style. Window seats offer a place to sit, with a mug of coffee, a book, or a pencil and notebook – a place to enjoy the present and watch the village life beyond. My love for Cornwall and France is combined with the love of bringing people together for good food and wine. Low lighting and rustic tables set the scene in the restaurant, a place to enjoy being together.

It takes a village community and the help of word of mouth for everyone to find the Inn through the narrow Cornish lanes. Two years ago, I converted the adjacent derelict barn into four beautiful rooms, again with a minimal style, with white linen sheets and bolster cushions and blankets giving a homely feel. They have proved a huge success, with guests being able to enjoy a rustic, countryside retreat amid the beauty Cornwall has to offer.

During my time at the St. Tudy Inn, I have been lucky enough to be recognised by the hospitality industry. A Michelin Bib Gourmand was thrilling to receive, and we have retained this since 2016. Being listed in The Estrella Damm Top 50 Gastropubs since 2016 has also been wonderful. Finding myself in CODE Hospitality's top 100 women was very humbling and appearing on television has been exhilarating.

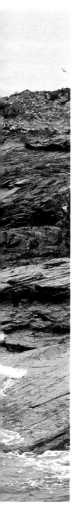

One of things I have enjoyed most during my time here is the people I have met along the way; from production teams to like-minded chefs, I have made friends for life. I am often asked what is it like to work in such a male-dominated industry. I think there is a misconception about there being a shortage of female chefs. I think women are more modest about how good they are and what they can achieve on their own and as part of a team. Long hours and huge pressure are part of the job, but if you love what you do it makes the journey a whole lot easier. I love the hustle and bustle of restaurant life and the non-stop world that is hospitality. The running of my team is hugely important to me, as is the feeling of capturing the heart of a community and being quietly consistent.

I sometimes wonder how I juggled family life and my work life. It was necessary to earn a living and it is what I do – I love to work and be creative. I have learned some hard lessons over the years and only now have I realised that a balance of creativity and business is very much needed. My children once said that I would have made a terrible stay-at-home mother (thanks, kids!).

Sadly, we lost Monty, our Labrador in summer 2019. Such a top dog and a constant support in everything I have done, I always had unconditional love from my dog. He always got me up and out on the darkest of days. In his honour, I collaborated with The Harbour Brewing Co. and created MONTY DOG ale on tap at the Inn. Monty is never forgotten, and a sea dog until the end. Inca, our spaniel, remains my partner-in-crime now and has become needier than ever and a constant trip hazard.

Our life here at the Inn reminds me of living in Blanot, a small provincial village deep in the heart of Burgundy. The community and the sense of place, the way of life – somewhat slower than that of the cities – feels the same. The importance of the land and what it provides, and the importance of a place to gather and be together. One of the only differences, perhaps, is that the French accents of Blanot are replaced by the gentle Cornish tones of my locals at the Inn. On Sunday afternoons in the summer, after lunch, I love hearing the laughter and clink of glasses as everyone plans their week ahead or discusses the latest gossip. It takes people to make a place.

RUSH SLOWLY – PORT ISAAC

A place that will always be part of my life is Port Isaac, a small fishing village on the Atlantic coast of North Cornwall. All at sea, the air, the sound of the waves, the cries of the seagulls – haunting and beautiful – are synonymous with coastal life. The vastness of the ocean always puts life into perspective – everything always seems better by the seaside. Port Isaac is Oscar, Finn and Evie's home; their idyllic upbringing by the sea has been one of the most wonderful things, and I count myself lucky in so many ways to have lived there for a decade.

Port Isaac is the place that drew me to this magical county and to a particular fisherman, too – or perhaps that should be the other way around. In my early years in Cornwall, I shared a life with John, or JB as he is known. Shanty songs, fishing and the rest, John is Port Isaac born and bred.

In our home by the sea in the wondrous village of PI is where my Cornish food journey began. Our kitchen was full of Cornishware, capturing warmth and the heart of the house – its nautical stripes with accents of sun-bleached colour channelled the spirit of living by the sea. It was reminiscent of a coastal-style kitchen way back when, and it was a home that felt all about us, and it reflected the breeziness of its seaside setting.

In PI, life is slow. Nothing is done in a rush. You either rush slowly or will be there 'dreckley'. That being said, we had a chaotic life with three children all under the age of three and our dog, Gunnel. We lived off the back of tourists' high days and holidays and the summer months were so important to help get through the long Cornish winter.

Cornwall feels like a country on its own. John always referred to it as 'God's Country'. From the moment you cross the border into the county (we always had a ritual with the children – we would close our eyes as we crossed and say 'piskies, piskies, piskies' three times over and 'I love you') it feels as though you are entering another world, a magical world, a world like no other, where holiday memories and moments are made, and that long journey seemed to be worth it. The Cornish have a fond nickname for outsiders: 'incomers' – or, less fondly, 'emmets' – as, yes, I will never be a local, even after a lifetime of calling this place home.

I arrived in Port Isaac in the late spring of 1999. We purchased a 4-storey, Grade II-listed house in the heart of the village, where the first two floors were a former shop, with Palladian windows and beautiful Cornish slate floors and ceiling beams. Our seaside café, Browns, opened in the spring of 2000, offering good coffee, homemade cakes and Port Isaac crab sandwiches, and the best Cornish ice cream and cream teas around. Back then, the winters were long in Cornwall and to survive them you had to work very hard from Easter until October. Browns was a much-loved shop at Victoria House, and I have very fond memories of our time there.

CORNWALL

I went on to open The Harbour No1 Middle Street restaurant in Port Isaac, which looks out to sea. A 15th-century fisherman's cottage with low ceilings and wonky walls, it was here that I fell in love with fish cookery, and where I quietly and consistently cooked for the next seven years. That small harbourside kitchen is where I learned many of my skills.

Fishing boats and harbours were always part of our life. Winnie the Pooh, LEJ and the Laura B were all boats of JB's over the years (apparently, I did not stick around long enough to have a boat named after me). I was also there for the early days of the shanty-singing group, the Fisherman's Friends, that John founded. There was nothing more idyllic than listening to the boys sing on a Friday, watching the sun set over Port Isaac harbour, then heading to The Golden Lion for more songs, and always the loveliest rendition of *Little Eyes*. Shanties will always have a place in my life and heart, as well as hearing 'Dear of 'er' said in a thick Cornish accent.

These are good memories, and JB and I have three wonderful children of whom we are very proud. We have no regrets. Life is not always easy or meant to be, but Port Isaac will always be a place I love. Thank you to John and to Laura (my step-daughter).

PORT ISAAC LORE FROM JOHN

'Fishermen do not swim', among other things, is one of those fishing superstitions that will continue to live on throughout the generations. I have always remained fond of some of these legends, especially no.1. I still never start anything new on a Friday.

1. Never start anything new on a Friday.

2. Green jumpers or green wellies are a no-go on board a fishing boat.

3. Do not discuss rabbits on board. If you do, you must refer to them as 'underground greyhounds'.

4. No whistling on board; it may muster up a gale.

5. First lobster of the season is always thrown back into the waters.

6. It is bad luck to see a vicar on land when you are aboard your boat about to go fishing.

7. Always get on or off the boat on the starboard side.

8. Port Isaac folk are referred to as 'Yarnie Goats' by folk from Padstow and Padstow folk are referred to as 'Town Crows'. Gentle rivalry.

A map, drawn by Mark Hellyar, my partner, of my favourite shoreline
and coves, and the places I call home here in Cornwall. Inland from
St. Tudy to the shores of Port Isaac, North Cornwall, heading west to
the coves of Pinehawn, Varley, Port Quin, Lundy Bay, Rumps, Polzeath,
Grenaway, Daymer, Rock, Porthilly, Padstow, Tregirls, Stepper Point,
Butterhole, Trevone, Harlyn Bay, Bloodhound, Greenclose Cove,
Boat Bay (Onjohn Cove), Tide Teller, Big Guns Cove and Cataclews.
There is no place like home.

EARLY YEARS

Growing up in the 1980s and early '90s was colourful. I have memories of our house always being full of laughter and music. It was the era of the classic dinner party – so sociable and fun. The kitchen was always the place we would find ourselves. The best parties always end up in the kitchen. I come from a large theatrical family, so my memories from a child's perspective, looking up, were always of laughter and merriment and trying to dodge the ash dropping from cigarettes above (it was fashionable and socially acceptable then to smoke).

I was an awkward child, slightly quirky. I think I probably still am. I am shy by nature, but was always drawn to the kitchen. Sunday mornings were often spent leaning into the Aga at home, watching my mother, who is a very good cook, make her roux for her white sauce. The rattle of the glass at the bottom of the pan as Ma heated the milk was a sign that it was ready, as you never wanted the milk to boil over (so she said). Adding the milk slowly to the roux and watching the sauce magically thicken; a teaspoon of English mustard, which always managed to make my eyes water; grating the Cheddar through a mouli; taking the sauce off the heat to add the cheese, salt and pepper, to taste. I was always allowed to lick the saucepan – such a wonderful memory – creamy and comforting with the warmth of mustard bringing out the flavour of the cheese. Looking back, I learned so much from my mother without even realising.

Cauliflower cheese was always a highlight for me, and so was making the gravy for Sunday lunch. Resting the meat then bringing all the juices, carrots, onions and herbs to a simmer in the pan. We added a stock cube back then, but I remember always being fascinated about the process. Another roux, then adding stock, red wine, Worcestershire sauce and water from the vegetables that were simmering away. Stirring, tasting, and considering flavours is something I love. I would sit up on the kitchen surface and watch, taste and learn, as my mother nourished us and brought us all together.

My mother's timing was always perfect. Plates put on to warm, table laid and lunch was always ready just as the end titles of *The Waltons* could be heard playing in the background on the small portable TV.

The kitchen was a comforting place, where all things seemed possible and everyone would eventually come together. The kitchen witnessed all the excitement of seeing family and friends, of celebrating surprise birthdays and anniversaries over the years, of Sunday lunches, summer holidays and Christmases. Whether I was scraping the leftovers from the cake bowl, making meringues or melting chocolate, there was always something to do and feel part of a sense of belonging.

A COOK AND
HER KITCHEN

My kitchen is where I feel most at home, where I feel confident and happiest. My cooking has changed over the years and now I think it is a true reflection of me and how I think and feel. Simple, seasonal and beautiful, the finesse I bring to my food has evolved over time, bringing me new confidence and delight. What I love about cooking is how creative it is and how much joy it brings to others – I think cooking for other people is one of the most loving of all human skills.

I cook with the ebb and the flow of the seasons, going effortlessly along with what nature has to offer at its best. I know where I am then. There is something grounding and reassuring about each changing season. I could not tell you which season is my favourite, but the promise of each one brings its own excitement, evokes different memories and brings different produce into my kitchen.

I have a small kitchen garden outside my kitchen door and there is nothing more lovely than being able to grow your own produce. Herbs inspire me and are essential to cook with. I love their scent, fragrance, colour, diversity and natural beauty. Along with herbs, you will always find butter, eggs, lemons, garlic, chilli, Cornish sea salt and good olive oil in my larder.

The simplicity of good oil, bread and sea salt is hard to beat. We always find ourselves pouring a couple of glugs of olive oil into a bowl, then adding sea salt and black pepper. Pieces of torn sourdough soak up the green oil – delicious with a glass of wine before supper. And with that comes the pop of the cork, smelling and tasting – considering wine is something that is always done in our house. Our home reflects who we are and what we love.

There is detail in everything I do. It is important to me to take time with flowers for the table, glassware, crockery, cutlery and napkins. It is like dressing a theatre set but without the drama. I aim for a look of effortless simplicity, and a sense of place and being.

I love nothing more than bringing people together around a table for food, wine and conversation. The table comes first. It is a place that, as a family, we have all our conversations, sharing our days, both good and challenging. It is a place to laugh and bicker over who does the washing up. There is no better place.

A SENSE OF PLACE

Food, for me, is not about meals as such, but about ingredients associated with a particular place, with a moment in time, with making memories...

Sipping wine as the sun sets over the vineyard in Civrac; white peaches on the balcony at Les Levriers in Frejus; a crab sandwich on the Platt in Port Isaac looking out to sea; strawberries in June eaten from the punnet; blackberries picked triumphantly in the late summer or early autumn with the promise of crumble and homemade custard; autumn days walking across the golden beaches at Harlyn and then hunkering down for a long lunch.

I am often asked what my last meal would be, and I think it would actually have to be just an ingredient associated with a place. Maybe seaweed, foraged from the Cornish shores... Or a peach, perhaps, eaten in Provence where my grandparents used to live, with the rolling hills of lavender, rosemary and thyme, the fragrant pine trees above and the familiar hum of the crickets. That will do.

KITCHEN NOTES AND ESSENTIAL RECIPES

MY CORNISH STORECUPBOARD

Knowing where my ingredients come from is so important to me. I am so lucky in Cornwall to have the most wonderful producers on my doorstep, who have become friends over the years. I have the best of both worlds, working inland and living by the sea. My food heroes are the farmers and fishermen who work so hard every day of the year in all weathers to bring produce to our tables.

The simple things in life bring me the most joy. Colour, texture and taste are paramount. So, having quality suppliers means everything to me – talking to them is a good way to learn about the food we are eating.

I will always use Cornish sea salt and freshly ground pepper, and always use medium, free-range eggs. Good olive oil is essential. I like to use fresh stock, but there are many good stocks you can buy, so do not get overwhelmed by making it. Always go for the best quality you can find. I use sustainable fish where I can. Here in Cornwall, I have many sources of the finest fish and shellfish. Always talk to your fishmonger.

TOOLS

Chopping board A chopping board, or two, is essential.

Saucepans A set of three saucepans of various sizes is a good idea, plus medium and large frying pans (skillets). You will also need a good size pot for making stocks and, of course, for cooking pasta.

Knives My knives bring me joy every day – they are beautiful, sophisticated and practical. If you are a keen cook, I would encourage you to invest in some good knives.

Apron I would never be without an apron. I love the way that they fit and there is a comfort in having a uniform. I was taught early on in my cooking career to tidy as you go. This is important to me, because if I feel organised, I feel a sense of creativity.

Plates For me, I feel that white plates always provide a blank canvas for my dishes. Stylish and simple, yet smart.

Cutlery Investing in good-quality cutlery makes all the difference when serving up your food. Laying the table with your best cutlery and napkins out, can make the dining-in experience feel so much more special.

Other indispensables Colanders, sieves, graters, wooden spoons, a ladle, spatulas, a mouli for puréeing and mashing and a pestle and mortar. Baking trays and a handheld electric whisk or KitchenAid stand mixer are essential for me when it comes to baking. Many of these things are an everyday part of every household, and there are multitude of gadgets on the market to satisfy everyone's needs.

For a full list of my recommended, go-to suppliers, see pages 244-245.

INGREDIENTS

Here is a glimpse of what you will always find in my storecupboard or refrigerator, while my fresh ingredients change with the different seasons. Remember to replace what you have used up when you go shopping – keep a list.

Citrus

Clotted cream

Coastal sea herbs

Cornish sea salt

Crème fraiche

Dark chocolate (54 per cent
  cocoa solids)

Edible flowers

Eggs (medium, organic
  free-range)

Garden herbs

Green things (kale, lettuce,
  spinach etc.)

Good olive oil

Good Parmesan

Grains

Honey

Nuts and seeds

Piment d'Espelette (Basque
  mild red pepper powder)

Rapeseed oil

Ready-made puff pastry

Risotto rice

Saffron

Soft brown sugar

Stone fruits

Tinned artichoke hearts

Tomatoes (never in the fridge)

Unsalted Cornish butter

Vanilla pods

These are just some of my favourite ingredients that I always keep in store. 'Essentials' are the ingredients you choose that should make you feel good – everyone's essentials will be different.

My larder at home is a treasure trove. I have often dreamed of having a walk-in larder, but instead, it is an antique cupboard, fronted with chicken wire and painted in Atelier Ellis' Garden Party Green (I am also slightly obsessed with their beautiful hue of white that is called Milk). It stands in my kitchen for dry stores and essential ingredients, and I could not be without it.

Lockdown has given me the chance to become a little obsessive – perhaps I ought to rephrase that – 'more organised', meaning that all my glass Kilner (Mason) storage jars, standing tall on old scaffolding boards in my kitchen, now all have tape labels (that black embossed tape that I used to use as a lover of stationery back in the '90s), giving clear instructions as to the contents, from granulated sugar to caster (superfine) to Demerara to soft brown... Oh, this has brought me so much happiness! Set on the self, they make an attractive display. I have even labelled the shelves in my airing cupboard... there is no stopping me!

I think that cooking becomes much more enjoyable and less of a chore if you have everything you need on hand to be spontaneous. Then, if you have the urge to bake a ginger cake, you already have ingredients like black treacle (molasses), golden syrup (light corn syrup) and ginger in your storecupboard. Cooking and baking should not be a chore, it should be a joyful, creative and nourishing experience. Time, I know, is precious these days, but I challenge you to try to make some time and try something new in your kitchen today, whether it is sorting out your larder or planning to bake once a week. It will make you feel good and give you a warm sense of achievement. Not forgetting the happiness you will bring to others.

HERBS AND WILDFLOWERS

Cooking would mean nothing to me without herbs – they are as essential in my kitchen as a bowl of lemons. Herbs always make me feel positively joyful – their colours, shapes and scents, they are so clever and diverse. I would encourage you to always have herbs somewhere in your house. On your kitchen windowsill or in pots outside your kitchen door, in window boxes to add a pop of colour and hopefulness to your home – place them where they are easily at hand.

Basil: With its summery, intense fragrance, it is always a herb I have on my kitchen windowsill. I always use it up quickly, as I tend not to be green-fingered enough to keep it alive for very long. Thai basil is also delicious and brings an aniseed flavour to dishes and elevates the look of the dish.

Borage: A wonderful herb that blooms with pretty edible flowers from spring to late summer. The flowers are often blue, although white can also be found. I use borage flowers as decoration in salads, cakes and puddings. For something different, put them in an ice-cube tray, fill with water and freeze – they bring a cool cucumber-like flavour to summertime drinks. The old name for borage is 'bee bread'. Bees and pollinating insects go wild for the nectar of the flowers.

Chives: Beautifully tall chives remind me of childhood days, of family summer parties with old-school potato salad with mayonnaise. It is always part of my *fines herbes* mixture, which also includes parsley and tarragon. There is something so comforting in being able to go outside to the kitchen garden and snip some for cooking. The flowers are delicious too, adding that delicious allium kick to any dish along with a pop of colour.

Coriander (cilantro): Fresh coriander is a herb that you either love or hate. I love it – so versatile and delicious in fish cookery. It grows well, although has a habit of bolting and reaching for the sky.

Edible Flowers: Life to me is all about colour, and cooking with edible flowers has always been a highlight. Nasturtiums, violas, wild garlic, scented pelargoniums, chive flowers, French marigolds, borage, strawberry blossom and chamomile. You eat with your eyes and, for me, a dish without flowers feels incomplete.

Fig Leaves: If you are lucky enough to have a fig tree in your garden, I would encourage you to use the leaves. I sometimes infuse them in milk and cream with a vanilla pod (bean) for my panna cotta recipe (see page 196). The fig leaves bring a delicate flavour of coconut, which is unbelievably good.

Lovage: Lovely lovage has a flavour that is a mixture between celery and parsley. Wonderful in cooking, it is a herb I have grown very fond of over time.

Mint: Medicinal and wonderful. Mint inspires me and always gives me a sense of well-being. Fresh mint tea is delicious and cleansing and a go-to tonic or cuppa. There are so many varieties, too. I particular like garden mint, chocolate mint and strawberry mint. Easy to grow, although it has a tendency to take over, so I tend to plant mine in pots in my planters.

Parsley: Always flat-leaf for me and always a herb I use to finish dishes, from omelettes to kedgeree. Once you start cooking with this herb you will never go back.

Rosemary: Steadfast and true, a herb that I love. Hardy, it requires little attention apart from a good dose of Cornish sunshine. It thrives particularly well by the sea. In the spring, beautiful blue flowers appear, which I use to decorate dishes or for making rosemary sugar to use in shortbread.

Sage: An earthy herb that I always associate with the colder months. I find sage particularly beautiful, such delicate leaves with an intense autumnal feel.

Tarragon: Sings summer to me. A herb that is often underrated and misunderstood, it is one of my favourite essentials (see page 43) and once you have made it you will need it in your life.

THICK VANILLA CUSTARD

CRÈME ANGLAISE OR ENGLISH CREAM
(JUST DELICIOUS)

Serves 8

Serves 8

1 vanilla pod
300 ml (10 fl oz/1¼ cups) double
   (heavy) cream
700 ml (24 fl oz/scant 3 cups) milk
4 egg yolks
100 g (3½ oz/scant ½ cup) caster
   (superfine) sugar
3 tablespoons cornflour (cornstarch)

Halve the vanilla pod and scrape out the seeds. Put both the pod and seeds in a large pan over a medium-low heat, pour in the cream and milk and bring just to the point of simmering. Remove from the heat and leave to cool slightly.

In a large mixing bowl, whisk the egg yolks with the sugar and cornflour until pale. Gradually add the warm milk mixture, a ladleful at a time, whisking well between each addition. Remove the vanilla pod and set aside (see note on page 38).

Place a sieve over the pan and pour the mixture back into the pan. Cook gently over a low heat for about 15 minutes until thickened, stirring continuously.

This is best served immediately, but if not, to prevent a skin forming on the top of the custard, place a wet piece of baking parchment over the surface.

'FOOD glorious food'... Oliver Twist by Charles Dickens.

I often had custard straight out of the tin as a child. These days though, I always make my own. This is a custard of dreams, which is essential in the colder months. So good.

500 ml (17 fl oz/2 cups) double
   (heavy) cream
1 vanilla pod, split
8 egg yolks
100 g (3½ oz/scant ½ cup) caster
   (superfine) sugar

Put the cream and the vanilla pod into a heavy-based saucepan over a medium-low heat and bring gently to a simmer. Remove from the heat and set aside to infuse for 10 minutes. Carefully remove the pod (bean) (see note on page 38) and carefully scrape the vanilla seeds into the cream – it will be hot.

Put the egg yolks and sugar in a large bowl and stir together. Pour the infused cream onto the egg yolks and sugar.

Set a sieve over a clean saucepan and pour the mixture into the pan. Cook over a low heat, stirring, until the cream coats the back of the spoon and the mixture slightly thickens. Be careful not to let it get too hot, as it will scramble.

Pour into a favourite jug and allow to chill, or eat straight from the pan.

CRÈME Anglaise. Cold or hot, essential for puddings, a jugful of creamy custard to pour over crumbles, cakes and tarts (almost over cereal, but perhaps that's going too far...).

SOFT, crumbly or chewy, fudge is the sweetest treat. This is such a good recipe – it was given to me by a friend who always pulled the most amazing supper parties together with effortless style. You do not visit Cornwall without searching for fudge. There is something so nostalgic about going into the fudge shop and, with childlike eyes, wide open, choosing and deciding on how much fudge you could actually eat. My eyes have always been bigger than my stomach! This is a no-faff, no-fuss recipe and you can easily leave the hazelnuts out.

CHOCOLATE AND HAZELNUT FUDGE

Makes 24 small squares

150 g (5 oz) good-quality dark
    chocolate (54 per cent cocoa solids)
1 x 250 g (9 oz) jar Nutella (chocolate
    hazelnut spread)
1 x 400 g (14 oz) tin condensed milk
50 g (2 oz/⅓ cup) roasted skinned hazelnuts,
    gently crushed
Cornish sea salt, for sprinkling

Bring a pan of water to a simmer. Place the chocolate, Nutella and condensed milk into a heatproof bowl and place it over the pan without letting it touch the water. Allow everything to gently melt together, then stir through the hazelnuts.

Meanwhile, line a square baking tin (pan) with baking parchment.

Pour the fudge mixture into the tin and chill in the refrigerator for at least 4 hours before cutting into squares. Top each piece of fudge with a little sprinkling of sea salt.

CRÈME CHANTILLY

GOLDEN SYRUP FLAPJACKS, GOOD FOR ANY DAY

Serves 8

Makes 24

300 ml (10 fl oz/1¼ cups) double (heavy) cream
2 tablespoons icing (confectioner's) sugar
1 vanilla pod (bean), split and seeds scraped out (see note below)

225 g (8 oz) unsalted butter, plus extra for greasing
225 g (8 oz/1 cup) Demerara sugar
4 tablespoons golden (light corn) syrup
350 g (12 oz/3½ cups) rolled oats

In a large bowl, whip the cream, icing sugar and vanilla seeds together until soft peaks form when the whisk is removed. Store in the refrigerator until ready to serve.

Note: Wash off your vanilla pod and dry it, then store in an airtight jar to reuse. I find that when they have dried completely I can whiz them up in a blender with some caster (superfine) sugar to make vanilla sugar, which I use in biscuits.

JOY DE VIVRE. *At L'Etape (see page 231), we would always have crème Chantilly on the menu. I could eat it straight from the bowl. A little more decadent than cream on its own, I use it for pavlovas, profiteroles, trifles and Eton mess. Sweetened cream with specks of vanilla running through it is one of life's joys.*

Preheat the oven to 180°C (160°C fan/350°F/Gas 4).

Butter a 30 x 23 cm (12 x 9 in) traybake or roasting tin (pan).

Melt the butter in a large saucepan along with the sugar and syrup until the sugar has dissolved and the mixture is well combined. Stir in the oats and mix well. Turn the mixture into the prepared tin and press flat with a palette knife or the back of a spoon.

Bake in the oven for about 35 minutes, or until pale golden brown.

Remove from the oven and leave to cool in the tin for 10 minutes. Mark into 24 squares and leave to finish cooling in the tin.

They will keep in an airtight container for up to 10 days. (Thank you, Amanda.)

NUTS about flapjacks. With the familiar smell of butter, syrup, brown sugar and oats, flapjacks are always a go-to treat for my children. After school or even for breakfast, they are comforting and almost good for you. Have one with a mug of tea and put the world to rights.

BROWN SUGAR SHORTBREAD STARS

AMARETTI CRUMBLE CRISP (A TOPPING FOR SO MANY THINGS)

Makes about 12

Serves 8–10

300 g (10½ oz) unsalted butter, softened
135 g (4½ oz/¾ cup) soft light brown sugar
420 g (15 oz/3⅓ cups) plain (all-purpose) flour, plus extra for dusting
caster (superfine) sugar, for sprinkling

160 g (5½ oz) amaretti biscuits
80 g (3 oz/scant 1 cup) flaked (slivered) almonds
75 g (2½ oz) unsalted butter, room temperature
50 g (2 oz/scant ½ cup) plain (all-purpose) flour
50 g (2 oz/¼ cup) caster (superfine) sugar

Preheat the oven to 170°C (150°C fan/340°F/Gas 3). Line a baking sheet with baking parchment.

In a large bowl, beat the softened butter and light brown sugar together until smooth. Sieve over the flour and mix until the mixture comes together into a smooth dough.

Turn out onto a lightly floured surface and use a rolling pin to gently roll the dough out to 1 cm (½ in) thick. Cut into rounds – I usually like to use a pretty star-shaped cutter – and place on the prepared baking sheet. Sprinkle with sugar and chill in the refrigerator for 15 minutes.

Transfer the sheet of shortbread to the oven and bake for 10–15 minutes until pale golden brown. Transfer to a wire rack to cool and sprinkle with more sugar.

Preheat the oven to 180°C (160°C fan/350°F/Gas 4).

In a food processor, blend the amaretti biscuits with the flaked almonds.

In a mixing bowl, rub the butter and flour together to resemble breadcrumbs, then add the sugar along with the almond crumble and mix together.

Spread the mixture out over a baking sheet and bake in the oven for 10–15 minutes until golden. Allow to cool.

Perfect topping for poached vanilla apricots, plums and apples, blackberries, pears or candy-pink rhubarb.

BAKING is something I have always loved (I have a sweet tooth). Baking biscuits is therapeutic to me; whenever I feel slightly off balance or down, baking brings me back up. Shortbread is a real favourite of mine and goes beautifully with my panna cotta recipe on page 196. To test I always break a biscuit in half and look in wonder at the clever short layers.

PUDDING! Give me pudding every day. I love fruit crumbles and pies and there is nothing better than making a sweet treat for the people you love. This recipe is so simple and versatile. I use it to top fruit throughout the seasons. It is lighter than a traditional oat crumble topping, and delicious with custard or ice cream.

A LOVELY recipe that is quick and easy to make, especially with children. The dough can be made in advance and freezes well. Nothing beats a homemade cookie.

DARK CHOCOLATE AND OAT COOKIES

Makes 20, plus dough to freeze for another day

125 g (4 oz) unsalted butter, softened
80 g (3 oz/scant ½ cup) light brown sugar
1 egg, beaten
50 g (2 oz/scant ½ cup) self-raising flour
125 g (4 oz/1¼cups) rolled oats
½ teaspoon baking powder
175 g (6 oz) dark chocolate (54 per cent
    cocoa solids), roughly chopped

Preheat the oven to 180°C (160°C fan/350°F/Gas 4). Line a baking sheet with baking parchment.

In a large bowl, cream the butter and sugar together until light and fluffy. Beat in the egg gradually, then stir in the remaining ingredients. Mix well.

Place teaspoonfuls of the mixture, spaced well apart, on the prepared baking sheet. Bake in the oven for 15 minutes.

Remove and transfer to a wire rack to cool.

Note: If you fancy making a larger batch to have some on standby for unexpected guests, the raw cookie dough freezes well in balls and can be cooked from frozen.

ROAST NEW POTATOES WITH THYME AND GARLIC

BUTTERED PEAS WITH PARSLEY AND CHIVES

Serves 4

Serves 4

1 kg (2 lb 4 oz) new potatoes, unpeeled
2–3 tablespoons olive oil
5 sprigs of fresh rosemary, leaves picked
5 sprigs of fresh thyme, leaves picked
10 garlic cloves, unpeeled
Cornish sea salt

500 g (1 lb 2 oz/3¼ cups) frozen peas
50 g (2 oz) unsalted butter
1 tablespoon chopped flat-leaf parsley
1 tablespoon chopped chives
Cornish sea salt

Preheat the oven to 200°C (180°C fan/400°F/Gas 6).

Rinse and dry the potatoes. Pour the olive oil into a roasting tin (pan) and put in the oven to heat up for 10 minutes. When the oil is hot, add the rosemary, thyme and garlic and stir in. Add the potatoes and toss well. Roast for 40–50 minutes until the potatoes are golden brown and tender. Sprinkle with sea salt.

Bring a pan of water to the boil and cook the peas for 3 minutes. Drain, add the butter, herbs and a pinch of sea salt. Serve immediately.

PEAS. I love peas. Peas with everything please, freshly podded or more often than not freshly frozen petit pois. I have a lovely memory as a child of always using my soft fluffy mash potato on my plate to pick my peas up on my fork, always served with my mother's roast chicken and lots of Aga gravy.

COMFORTING. Nothing is more delicious than small, soft skinned potatoes that crisp up beautifully in the oven with thyme and garlic. Rich and sweet they will leave you wanting to eat them straight from the tray. A variety you must try are 'Cornish earlies' in the Springtime; lightly wash, boil, add a generous amount of butter, Cornish sea salt and your favourite herbs, chopped.

GLAZED CARROTS

TARRAGON MAYO

Serves 4

Serves 6

8 carrots, peeled and sliced into rounds
1–2 tablespoons honey
50 g (2 oz) unsalted butter
1 thyme sprig, leaves picked
zest of 1 lemon
Cornish sea salt and freshly ground
    black pepper

3 egg yolks
juice of 1 lemon
1 teaspoon Dijon mustard
250 ml (8½ fl oz/1 cup) sunflower oil
a handful of fresh tarragon
Cornish sea salt and freshly ground
    black pepper

Place the carrots in a saucepan with
enough water to just cover them. Add the
honey, butter and thyme and a pinch of
sea salt. Place over a medium heat and
bring to the boil, then reduce to a simmer
and cook for 10 minutes until tender.

Place the egg yolks in a food processor
and add the lemon juice, mustard and
a good pinch of sea salt. Whiz until just
combined. With the motor still running,
slowly pour the oil through the funnel
in a fine, slow stream until all the oil is
incorporated and it has emulsified.

Increase the heat and boil rapidly to
reduce the remaining liquid to a sweet
shiny glaze. Just before serving, sprinkle
over the lemon zest and season to taste.

Remove the tarragon leaves from the
stalks and roughly chop. As you chop,
the delicious fragrance will be released.
Fold through the mayo, taste and season
as needed.

*SWEET and buttery, this is a classic way of
cooking carrots that I always do. Sprigs of
thyme and lemon zest always lift this humble
side dish. Batons or Chanternay, not school
cut rounds for me.*

OTHER VARIATIONS:
Saffron – dissolve 2 pinches of saffron in
2 tablespoons hot water, then stir through
the mayo (this is delicious with my Saffron
Fish Stew, see page 220).

Aïoli – add 2 puréed garlic cloves.

Citrus – add the zest of 1 lemon
and 1 lime.

*DELICIOUS with hints of liquorice and vanilla,
yet tarragon is sometimes a forgotten herb.
Once you have made this mayo, you will
always want to eat it with your roast chicken.*

ESSENTIAL, ESSENTIAL TOMATO SAUCE

GREEN SAUCE FOR EVERYTHING, OR SALSA VERDE

Makes 1 litre (34 fl oz/4 cups)

Makes 250 g (9 oz/1 cup)

2 tablespoons olive oil
1 onion, finely chopped
2 garlic cloves, finely sliced
1 bunch basil
4 x 400 g (14 oz) tins good-quality
    chopped tomatoes
1 bay leaf
2 tablespoons brown sugar
Cornish sea salt and freshly ground
    black pepper

2 garlic cloves
2 tablespoons fine capers
1 tablespoon gherkins
6 anchovy fillets
1 bunch flat-leaf parsley
1 bunch mint leaves
1 tablespoon Dijon mustard
3 tablespoons cider vinegar
90 ml (3 fl oz/6 tablespoons)
    good olive oil, or to taste
Cornish sea salt and freshly ground
    black pepper

Heat the olive oil in a large saucepan over a medium heat, add the onion and garlic and gently cook until soft and translucent, stirring occasionally. Tear in the basil, leaves, stalks and all. Empty the tins of tomatoes into the pan, add the bay leaf and sugar and stir together. Bring to the boil and then reduce the heat and simmer gently for 20–25 minutes.

Remove the pan from the heat and carefully remove the bay leaf. Pass the sauce through a sieve or place into a food processor and blend until smooth. If you prefer, you can leave the sauce rustic. Taste and season with salt and black pepper.

You can use the sauce immediately or it will keep in the refrigerator for up to a week. Alternatively, freeze it for another day in batches.

SIMPLE and essential in my kitchen. Make a batch and you will also have a base for so many dishes. It freezes beautifully, too. A delicious supper of tomato sauce, pasta, Parmesan and basil leaves is sometimes all I need.

Finely chop the garlic, capers, gherkins, anchovies and herbs. Although it is tempting to whiz all the ingredients in a blender, a much nicer texture is achieved with chopping by hand.

Mix the chopped ingredients with the mustard, vinegar and olive oil, adjusting the amount of olive oil to your preferred consistency. Season to taste. Store in a Kilner (Mason) jar in the refrigerator for up to 1 week.

COLOUR is important to me. This green sauce works well with so many things and you will always reach for it. To me, this is as essential as mustard or sea salt.

*MOREISH and perfect with a pre-dinner drink or on a picnic.
One is never enough.*

PARMESAN AND THYME PUFF PASTRY TWISTS

Makes 12

100 ml (3½ fl oz/scant ½ cup) good olive oil
2 tablespoons fresh thyme leaves,
    plus extra for sprinkling
small pinch of Cornish sea salt
1 x 375 g (13 oz) ready-rolled puff pastry sheet
50 g (2 oz) Parmesan, grated

Preheat the oven to 180°C (160°C fan/350°F/Gas 4). Line a baking sheet with baking parchment.

In a small bowl, combine the oil and thyme leaves and season with the sea salt.

Unroll the pastry sheet, brush it all over with the olive oil mixture and cut into 12 strips, each about 2.5 cm (1 in) wide or pencil thin. Sprinkle over the grated Parmesan and some more thyme leaves, then carefully twist each strip and place on the baking sheet.

Bake in the oven for 5–10 minutes until golden.

I like to line small terracotta flower pots with baking parchment and stand the twists in them to serve as an appetiser. They are delicious when still warm.

TEA parties are a quintessential way of life by the sea. Nothing says summer more than a cucumber sandwich. They are surprisingly delicious, as cucumber on its own can be rather bland.

Oscar, my eldest, born in late August, always celebrated his birthdays in the garden or on the beach, come rain or shine. There would be an old-fashioned spread of sandwiches, cheese and pineapple, scones with clotted cream and jam, mini sponge cakes, Little Gem biscuits, Jammy Dodgers and Twiglets. I would somehow always muster up a wonderful cake, from a tank one year to a castle the next, and then there was the ice-cream fort framed with chocolate flakes. The cucumber sandwich has found its way into my book quite unexpectedly, but it definitely deserves its place.

ENGLISH CUCUMBER SANDWICHES WITH SALTED BUTTER

Serves 6

1 cucumber, peeled and very thinly sliced
12 thin slices of a good square-shaped loaf
salted butter, softened, for spreading
2 tablespoons poppy seeds
Cornish sea salt and freshly ground black pepper
watercress and borage flowers, to garnish

Place the cucumber slices in a colander and sprinkle with a pinch of salt. Mix together and set in the sink to drain for 30 minutes.

Butter each slice of bread generously. Layer half of the slices of bread with cucumber slices and sprinkle a little black pepper on top. Close the sandwiches and trim off the crusts. Cut into fingers, scatter with poppy seeds and serve with watercress and borage flowers.

COMFORTING There is something so good about leeks and cheese together. They're so sweet and tender – I love leeks. My mother used to poach them, wrap them in ham and then pour over a delicious creamy cheese sauce – perhaps a little dated now and not something I have tried to recreate, personally preferring this simple recipe. Nothing else is really needed, although it eats perfectly with a pint of Monty Dog.

KEEN'S CHEDDAR ON TOAST WITH SWEET LEEKS

Serves 4

1 large leek, thinly sliced into rounds
50 g (2 oz) unsalted butter
1 heaped tablespoon plain (all-purpose) flour
250 ml (8½ fl oz/1 cup) double (heavy) cream
100 g (3½ oz) Keen's Cheddar (or any good-quality
    strong Cheddar), coarsely grated
1 tablespoon Dijon mustard
Cornish sea salt and freshly ground
    black pepper
4 slices of your favourite bread

Thoroughly wash the leek slices and pat dry.

Melt the butter in a large frying pan (skillet) over a low heat, add the leek and cook for 10–15 minutes until softened. Stir in the flour and continue to cook for a couple of minutes, then pour in the cream. Add the grated cheese and mustard, then season with a little salt and black pepper.

Meanwhile, preheat the grill (broiler) to high, and line a baking sheet with baking parchment.

Place the bread slices on the baking sheet and toast under the grill until golden. Turn the bread over, spoon over the leek and cheese mixture and return to the grill. Cook until the leek and cheese topping is golden.

Note: This is also delicious topped with watercress and finely sliced spring onions (scallions), dressed in some good olive oil.

PORT ISAAC crab is a delicious sustainable catch and is some of the finest shellfish you will find around the rocky shores. Cornwall would not be Cornwall without crab. I have spent much time watching the fishermen fishing off the shores of Port Isaac and waiting for the boats to come in with their haul. Crab is at its best from April to October.

These crab bruschetta make lovely little plates to share.

PORT ISAAC CRAB, TOAST AND MAYO

Serves 4

1 garlic clove, crushed
2–3 tablespoons good olive oil
4 slices of sourdough bread
grated zest of 1 lemon, then
    cut in half for squeezing
2 tablespoons good-quality mayonnaise
250 g (9 oz) fresh white crab meat, picked
    through to check for pieces of shell
100 g (3½ oz) micro basil leaves
Cornish sea salt and freshly ground black pepper
rocket (arugula), to serve

Preheat the oven to 180°C (160°C fan/350°F/Gas 4).

Mix the garlic with the olive oil and brush the surface of the bread with the mixture. Place on a baking sheet and toast in the oven for a few minutes until lightly golden and crisp.

Combine the lemon zest, mayonnaise and crab meat. Stir through the micro basil leaves and season well. Spoon the crab mixture over each slice of bread and serve immediately with rocket leaves and a squeeze or two of lemon juice.

WINTER
SEAS

WINTER SEAS (A SHANTY SONG TO FILL YOUR HEART)

WINTER WALKS early in the morning are so wonderful. This is just the beginning of one of my favourite times of the year. Allow yourself to enjoy the ordinary. Shades of the sea front, winter light that captures every moment in time, fishing boats leaving port headed out to work come rain or shine, the familiar sound of the ferry at rush hour. I am always wrapped up by the sea, walking past the tamarisk tree onto Boat Bay (Onjohn Cove), the cold winds, the swell of the ocean breaking on the shore in heavy, rolling billows, heading towards the dark clouds and the stormy seas. Bright but biting days.

I always embrace the winter, the blackened sky and thinking about my day ahead upon the dawn sands. If I ever need to clear my head or feed my soul, this is where you will find me. Half-lit grey days, a chill in the air, smoky evenings, Bonfire Night, Hallowe'en, the promise of Christmas ahead. Time to slow down with one-pot suppers, comfort food, or nursery puddings, in layers of my favourite oversized knitwear, hunkering down by the fire. Finding time for the simple pleasures: reading a book, finishing that puzzle, writing a letter, pottering in the garden, writing recipes, baking a cake, spending time and taking a moment to breathe. Kettle on.

GOOD MORNING! Another day ahead. I am a person of routine, although I love to hate it. Breakfast is always an important meal of the day but one that can often be overlooked. Over the years, my granola recipe has changed depending on my larder ingredients. The whole and ground almonds give a depth of flavour. This recipe is one of my favourites – accompanied with raspberries, Greek yoghurt and a squeeze of honey or two. Life is sweet.

GRANOLA WITH ALMONDS AND PECANS

Serves 10

450 g (1 lb/3½ cups) rolled oats
100 g (3½ oz/⅔ cup) whole almonds,
   roughly chopped
75 g (2½ oz/⅔ cup) ground almonds (almond meal)
75 g (2½ oz/¾ cup) pecans, roughly chopped
75 g (2½ oz/½ cup) pumpkin seeds
1 teaspoon ground cinnamon
125 g (4 oz/generous ⅓ cup) runny honey
50 ml (1¾ fl oz/3 tablespoons) vegetable oil
finely grated zest of 1 orange
1 vanilla pod (bean), split and seeds scraped out

Preheat the oven to 160°C (140°C fan/325°F/Gas 3). Line two large baking trays (pan) with baking parchment.

In a large bowl, mix together the oats, almonds, pecans, pumpkin seeds and cinnamon. Set aside.

Put the honey and oil into a small pan and heat gently until very liquid, about 30 seconds. Stir in the orange zest and vanilla seeds, then pour over the oat mixture in the bowl and mix thoroughly.

Divide the mixture between the baking trays and spread out evenly. Bake in the oven for 20–30 minutes, stirring once, until golden and toasted. Leave to cool completely before bagging or storing in an airtight container for up to 6 months.

CHANGE is in the air, autumn days have arrived and breakfast becomes very much fuel for the day. I love gently roasting plums with vanilla, bay and Demerara sugar. Sweet, glossy and rich in colour, they sit perfectly on my morning porridge. Blackberry compote works well with this, as does my Candy Pink Rhubarb Compote on page 136, or sometimes porridge simply on its own is all I need. I grew up in the days of the Ready Brek ads and the idea that you could go to school with a red glow around you. Of course, now I would find Ready Brek far too sweet, but the fun of making the well in the middle, then slowly adding the milk to watch it thicken, was magic.

PORRIDGE, GOLD TOP MILK, DEMERARA AND ROASTED PLUMS WITH BAY AND VANILLA

Serves 4

160 g (5½ oz/1¼ cups) organic rolled
   (porridge) oats
600 ml (20 fl oz/2½ cups) Gold Top
   or full-fat (whole) milk
pinch of Cornish sea salt

For the roasted plums
6 plums, halved and stoned (pitted)
1 bay leaf
1 vanilla pod (bean), split and seeds scraped out
100 ml (3½ fl oz/scant ½ cup) water
4 tablespoons Demerara sugar,
   plus extra for sprinkling

Begin with roasting the plums. Preheat the oven to 200°C (180°C fan/400°F/Gas 6).

Fit the plum halves into a small roasting tin (pan), cut-side up. Add the bay leaf and vanilla pods and seeds to the water, then pour around the plums. Sprinkle over the sugar. Roast in the oven for 25–30 minutes until the plums are soft but still holding their shape.

To make the porridge, place the oats and milk in a saucepan over a medium heat and add a pinch of sea salt. Bring it to a steady simmer and cook for 6–7 minutes, continuously stirring with a wooden spoon to give a smooth glossy finish.

Divide the porridge among serving bowls, top with the roasted plums and finish with a sprinkle of Demerara sugar.

YES to cake. Teatime treat or perfect pudding, this is a firm favourite in our house. The pistachios are like shining jewels on top of the cake, gently caramelised with citrus zest. It doesn't get much better.

PISTACHIO NUT PUDDING

Serves 8

250 g (9 oz) unsalted butter, softened
225 g (8 oz/1 cup) caster (superfine) sugar
zest of 1 lemon
zest of 1 lime
4 eggs
100 g (3½ oz/1 cup) ground almonds (almond meal)
100 g (3½ oz/1 cup) ground pistachios, skin on
50 g (2 oz/scant ½ cup) plain (all-purpose) flour
1 teaspoon baking powder

For the glaze
100 g (3½ oz/scant ½ cup) caster (superfine) sugar
zest of 1 lemon, plus 2 tablespoons juice
zest and juice of 1 lime
50 g (2 oz/⅓ cup) shelled pistachios

To serve
icing (confectioner's) sugar, for dusting
Crème Anglaise (see page 35)

Preheat the oven to 180°C (160°C fan/350°F/Gas 4). Butter and line a 900 g (2 lb) loaf pan with baking parchment.

In a large bowl, cream together the butter and sugar until light and fluffy, then stir in the lemon and lime zest. Whisk the eggs in a separate bowl, then slowly add them, whisking until incorporated.

Whiz the almonds and pistachios together in a food processor, then add the flour and baking powder and whiz to combine. Fold into the butter, egg and sugar mixture.

Spoon the mixture into the prepared loaf pan and bake in the oven for 30–40 minutes until golden brown and firm to the touch. Remove and leave to cool in the pan for about 10 minutes, then turn out onto a wire rack to cool completely.

For the glaze, put the sugar and lemon and lime juice into a heavy-based saucepan, and gently heat until the sugar has dissolved. Add the shelled pistachios and lemon and lime zest and simmer gently until a glaze forms.

Top the cooled cake with the glaze and dust lightly with icing sugar. Serve with jugfuls of Crème Anglaise (see page 35).

DELICATE and sweet. Here, a flat, white-fleshed fish is cooked simply with some of my favourite ingredients. Serve with steamed greens and Cornish new potatoes.

Check the fish for small bones and use tweezers to pull out any that you find. Always talk to your fishmonger – they are experts and will prepare the fish for you. Fish cookery is so exciting.

LEMON SOLE, HERB DRESSING, WATERCRESS AND SEA HERBS

Serves 2

4 x 150 g (5 oz) lemon sole fillets, skin on
good olive oil, for drizzling
a handful of flat-leaf parsley leaves,
    finely chopped
zest and juice of 1 lemon
½ garlic clove, finely chopped
Cornish sea salt

To serve
a handful of watercress and sea herbs
    (foraged or go to Bello Wild Food)
4 edible flowers, such as violas
steamed greens of choice
cooked Cornish new potatoes

Preheat the oven to 180°C (160°C fan/350°F/Gas 4). Line a baking sheet with baking parchment.

Place the sole fillets, skin-side down, on the lined baking sheet, drizzle with olive oil and season with a little salt. Bake in the oven for 4–5 minutes until the flesh is opaque and flakes easily. Remove from the oven and let rest for a few minutes.

In a small bowl, stir together the parsley, lemon zest and juice, and garlic with another drizzle of olive oil. Taste and consider the balance of flavours.

Place the sole fillets onto warmed serving plates and drizzle the herb dressing over the fish. Decorate with watercress and edible flowers and serve with steamed greens and new potatoes. Deliciously simple.

Note: I love using edible flowers in my cooking – a viola finishes off this dish beautifully.

HEARTY and the most comforting dish of all. I am transported back to deepest Burgundy with this slow-cooked beef. I love autumn and winter in Cornwall. The beaches appear almost deserted after the busy summer and we all start reaching for more one-pot suppers. This is always top of my list. Beach walks and seaside air will build your appetite for the king of stews.

BOEUF BOURGUIGNON, CHESTNUT MUSHROOMS, LARDONS WITH WINTER HERBS

Serves 6

2 tablespoons olive oil
900 g (2 lb) steak, cut into 4 cm (1½ in) chunks
1 onion, roughly chopped
1 heaped tablespoon plain (all-purpose) flour
450 ml (15 fl oz/1¾ cups) red wine
bouquet garni made up of 1 bunch thyme, 1 bunch rosemary
　　and 1 bay leaf, tied together
10 garlic cloves, peeled
350 g (12 oz) small shallots, peeled
125 g (4 oz) unsmoked bacon, cut into lardons
100 g (3½ oz) small button or chestnut
　　(cremini) mushrooms
Cornish sea salt and freshly ground
　　black pepper
good-quality bread of your choice, to serve

In a large casserole dish (Dutch oven), heat 1 tablespoon of the oil over a medium-high heat. Add the beef in batches and sear until dark brown on all sides. Do not overcrowd the pan. Use a slotted spoon to remove the beef to a plate and set aside.

Add the onion to the casserole dish and soften until golden brown. Return the meat to the pan and sprinkle over the flour, stirring to soak up the juices. Gradually pour in the red wine, stirring gently. Add the *bouquet garni* to the casserole, then add the garlic cloves, and season with salt and pepper. Place the lid on the dish and cook very gently over a low heat for 2 hours. Stir occassionally so it does not stick.

Heat the remaining tablespoon of oil in a frying pan (skillet) and fry the whole shallots and bacon lardons until lightly coloured.

After 2 hours, add the shallots, lardons and whole mushrooms to the casserole, stir and leave to cook for a further 1 hour. Check for seasoning then serve, spooned into bowls with hunks of bread.

Often misunderstood, fennel tends to divide people – you either love it or you hate it – but it always has a place in my kitchen. Comforting and delicious, this is a great recipe to try if you are not quite sure about this bulb. Tucked up here with butter, garlic and nutmeg, it offers a lighter dish to that of a potato gratin or one that has cream running through it, so give it a try. The delicate aniseed flavour is a perfect accompaniment to fish and chicken dishes, or it makes a quick and easy Sunday supper. To me, fennel is as good cooked as it is eaten raw (I think I have said that before!). I simply love it.

FENNEL AND PARMESAN GRATIN

Serves 4

4 large fennel bulbs, fronds trimmed and reserved
80 g (3 oz) butter
2 garlic cloves, thinly sliced
1 whole nutmeg, for grating
50 g (2 oz) Parmesan, grated
50 g (2 oz/generous ½ cup) sourdough breadcrumbs
Cornish sea salt and freshly ground black pepper

Preheat the oven to 200°C (180°C fan/400°F/Gas 6).

Bring a large saucepan of water to the boil. Trim the fennel, chopping off the bases and pulling away the thicker outer layers, then cut the bulbs into wedges. Add to the pan and boil for about 5 minutes until tender. Drain well.

In a separate large pan, melt the butter with the garlic over a low heat. Remove from the heat, add the fennel wedges and stir until coated, then add the reserved fennel fronds and season with grated nutmeg, salt and pepper, to taste.

Transfer the fennel mixture to an ovenproof dish. Stir the Parmesan and breadcrumbs together and sprinkle over the top. Bake in the oven for 15–20 minutes until golden.

CHICKEN WITH ORANGE,
CREAM AND TARRAGON

Serves 4

4 skinless, boneless chicken breasts, cut into strips
plain (all-purpose) flour, for dusting
25 g (1 oz) unsalted butter
1 tablespoon olive oil
100 g (3½ oz) tarragon, leaves stripped
    and roughly chopped
150 ml (5 fl oz/scant ⅔ cup) chicken stock
200 ml (7 fl oz/scant 1 cup) fresh orange juice
2 oranges, peeled and segmented
    (reserve the juices)
150 ml (5 fl oz/scant ⅔ cup) double (heavy) cream
Cornish sea salt and freshly ground black pepper

Pat the chicken strips dry with paper towels. Place some flour
for dusting in a bowl and season with salt and pepper. Add the
chicken strips to the bowl and toss to coat in the seasoned flour.

Heat the butter and oil in a medium frying pan (skillet) over a
medium heat. Add the chicken strips in batches and fry until brown
on all sides. Add a generous amount of the tarragon, reserving
a little for garnish. Add the stock and orange juice to cover the
chicken and simmer gently until the chicken is cooked through,
about 10 minutes.

Lift the chicken out of the pan and put in a shallow serving dish
along with the orange segments. Keep warm.

Continue to simmer the stock until reduced by half, then add the
cream and reduce again until you have a thick sauce. Taste, season
and add some of the reserved juices from the orange segments if
it needs to be sharpened.

Spoon the sauce over the chicken and garnish with the reserved
tarragon.

INSPIRING. One of my first cooking jobs when I returned from France was working for the formidable Penny Ide-Smith. I say formidable, she really was, and by that I mean driven, ambitious, fiercely hard working and an exceptionally good chef. I think, without even realising it, Penny gave me the experience I needed to thrive in a tough male-dominated industry. So this is a thank-you to Penny for giving me an opportunity to learn and cook. I will always be grateful to you for believing in me.

This recipe will always remind me of working with Penny. It's such a delicious combination of flavours and it celebrates tarragon, which in my mind is always a good thing. This dish works well throughout the year, although citrus always brings the sun to cold days.

Cornish pasty (mug of tea)

'ANSOME. There is nothing better than the waft of a Cornish pasty straight from the oven. Beef skirt is traditionally used for Cornish pasties, as it cooks in the same amount of time as the vegetables. A waxy potato, like a Wilja, is best to use, as it will not disintegrate. The pastry can be shortcrust, rough puff or puff. Crimping essential. This is the best form of comfort food on a grey day. I always eat mine with a mug of tea and ketchup on the side.

A simple question: Who makes the best pasty? This query always starts up a passionate debate among the fine people of Cornwall. Who is fuelling the South West with the best pasty? Where are the best places to buy a 'ansome pasty?

My favourite pasty shops:

Auntie Avice's Pasty Shop, St. Kew Highway
  (bloody lovely)

Mcfadden's, St. Just (the best down west)

Stein's Patisserie, Padstow (classy)

Malcom Barnecutt Bakery, Rock (consistently good)

Nicky B's Pasty Shop, Port Isaac (alright maid)

LOST BREAD. In my village of Blanot, we always used up the leftover baguettes to make this pudding. French bread is so good to use as the crust caramelises beautifully. I think that I will always be very fond of vanilla-y soaked bread and caramelised crusts – they bring such joy and happiness to me. My eyes are always bigger than my stomach, but I will always find a way for that second helping.

Bread and butter pudding is the most unctuous and delicious of all nursery puddings. There are, of course, many variations, using brioche, hot cross buns, chocolate, booze, marmalade and fruits of the seasons. Here, I have kept it simple with a classic version.

PAIN PERDU (LOST BREAD) PUDDING

Serves 6

100 g (3½ oz) unsalted butter, softened, plus
 extra for greasing
1 baguette, thinly sliced
350 ml (12 fl oz/1½cups) full-fat (whole) milk
150 ml (5 fl oz/scant ⅔ cup) double (heavy) cream
4 eggs
75 g (2½ oz/scant ⅓ cup) caster (superfine) sugar
grated zest of 1 orange
2 teaspoons Demerara sugar
2 apples (I love russet apples), peeled and sliced
vanilla ice cream or 250 ml (8½ fl oz/1 cup) single
 (light) cream, to serve

Preheat the oven to 180°C (160°C fan/350°F/Gas 4). Lightly butter a deep 18 x 23 cm (7 x 9 in) baking dish.

Generously butter the baguette slices on one side. Arrange the slices in a the baking dish, buttered-side up, overlapping each other and standing almost upright

Whisk together the milk, cream, eggs and sugar and pour the mixture all over the bread. Scatter the surface of the pudding with the grated orange zest, Demerara sugar and sliced apples, then bake on the top shelf of the oven for 35–40 minutes until it is puffy and golden and the top crust is crunchy.

Serve the pudding straight from the oven, either with vanilla ice cream or chilled pouring cream.

GOLDEN. I give you a different kind of sunshine to brighten up your day – my citrusy lemon tart. Sharp and sweet, with the mascarpone giving it a delicious creamy texture. I like to serve it with a dollop of clotted cream or crème fraîche. I am a little obsessed with lemons – for must-read book inspiration, read The Land Where Lemons Grow *by Helena Attlee.*

WINTER CITRUS TART

Serves 10

For the sweet pastry
350 g (12 oz/2¾ cups) plain (all-purpose) flour
pinch of Cornish sea salt
225 g (8 oz) cold unsalted butter, cut into pieces
100 g (3½ oz/generous ¾ cup) icing (confectioner's) sugar
3 egg yolks

For the filling
zest and juice of 6 lemons
6 eggs, plus 6 egg yolks
350 g (12 oz/1½ cups) caster (superfine) sugar
300 g (10½ oz/1¼ cups) mascarpone
2 tablespoons icing (confectioner's) sugar, to decorate

For the pastry, put the flour, salt and butter into a food processor and pulse to the texture of coarse breadcrumbs. Add the icing sugar and egg yolks, then pulse into a soft ball. Wrap in cling film (plastic wrap) and chill in the refrigerator for 1 hour.

Preheat the oven to 150°C (130°C fan/300°F/Gas 1).

Coarsely grate the pastry into a 26 cm (10 in) loose-bottomed fluted flan tin, then press it down evenly to cover the sides and base. Line with baking parchment and fill with baking beans. Bake blind for 20 minutes. Remove and set aside to cool then remove the beans.

Reduce the oven to 140°C (120°C fan/275°F/Gas ½)

For the filling, combine the lemon zest and juice in a bowl. In a separate bowl, beat the whole eggs and extra yolks together with the sugar. Add the mascarpone, stir to combine, then stir into the lemon mixture. Pour into the cooled tart shell and bake for 1 hour.

Remove and leave to cool, then sprinkle lightly with icing sugar before serving.

NOËL –
SMALL
WONDERS

CHRISTMAS (THE MOODY DAYS OF JANUARY BLUES & FEBRUARY GREYS)

NOËL. A time to celebrate. Taking a seat by the window is sometimes all I need, finding that winter light and looking out beyond – pencil and notebook in hand – coffee, candles and being cosy. A window seat gives me time to consider all the details, from styling my home to buying presents and how to wrap them, deciding what to cook and making that shopping list. Paper snowflakes hang over our table; there will be a bowl of clementines, a tin of Quality Street chocolates and Christmas carols on repeat. I love gold chocolate coins, stockings fireside, baking mince pies, my rich chocolate roulade with gold leaves, watching my favourite festive film, writing Christmas cards... all the childlike excitement, traditions and being together with the people I love, heart-to-heart.

As Christmas passes and the New Year appears, I enjoy the moment. I have all the feelings for January and February, moody but with the promise of spring ahead. I reach for the blues of the seaside as a mood-booster and for that much-needed daily dose of 'vitamin sea'. Indoors, the cow parsley I have dried in big vases with their beautiful long stems and black seeds, reminds me of lighter days to come. Humble potted plants are brought inside to decorate my tables and bring a palette of greens to chase away the winter blues.

This chapter will bring you home comfort and simplicity; warmth and colour to grey days; a chance for you to try ingredients you might have forgotten about; layered in time, a walk through the seasons, and an insight into what I hold dear.

Cooking with my children has always been a passion, as cooking brings us together and something to share together at the end of it. First jobs in the kitchen should be fun and memorable: peeling apples, podding beans and hulling strawberries. I have always thought that cooking builds self-esteem (and is great for maths skills). Although I have always been taught to tidy as you go in the kitchen, I try to let go and let the children be creative – even if that means more mess! As a self-confessed control freak, this has been challenging at times, but letting go can be incredibly therapeutic. Together, we make timeless festive creations, from baking to decorations: orange clove pomanders (see page 98), paper chains, dried orange garlands (see page 90), snowflake shortbread, mince pies, gingerbread bunting and a chocolate yule log.

NEVER rush an onion. I love these moreish, sweet tartlets that I always make at Christmastime. Onions need time – time to naturally sweeten and soften. It really is worth making your own shortcrust pastry. It can be made ahead and it freezes really well. Store-bought is good though, so don't worry if you don't have enough time.

VULSCOMBE GOAT'S CHEESE AND CARAMELISED RED ONION TARTLETS

Makes 24

250g (9 oz) ready-made shortcrust pastry
2 tablespoons olive oil
2 medium red onions, sliced
1 garlic clove, thinly sliced
1 teaspoon chopped thyme
1 teaspoon red wine vinegar
2 tablespoons soft light brown sugar
125g (4 oz) Vulscombe goat's cheese,
    cut into 24 small pieces
Cornish sea salt and freshly ground black pepper

Preheat the oven to 200°C (180°C fan/400°F/Gas 6).

Roll the pastry out to 2.5 mm (⅛ in) thick. Use a 5 cm (2 in) pastry cutter to cut 24 circles from it.

Place the circles onto a baking sheet and prick all over with a fork. Bake in the oven for 10–12 minutes, or until cooked through and golden-brown. Remove from the oven and set aside to cool.

Heat the oil in a frying pan (skillet) over a low heat, add the onions and gently fry for 15 minutes. Never rush an onion. Increase the heat, add the garlic and thyme and cook for a further 5 minutes. Add the vinegar and brown sugar and cook, stirring well, until the onions have caramelised. Season to taste with salt and pepper.

To assemble the tartlets, spoon some of the red onion mixture onto each pastry circle and top with a piece of cheese.

TRADITIONAL. Smoked salmon and lemon butter, tucked up in wholemeal bread, always brings much pleasure to any party. This is a perfect get-ahead canapé, which is a quality especially needed at Christmastime. You can prepare these a day in advance and keep them in the refrigerator.

SMOKED SALMON PINWHEELS

Makes 40 pinwheels

zest of 1 lemon
50 g (2 oz) butter, softened
4 slices of brown bread, crusts trimmed
100 g (3½ oz) smoked salmon slices
freshly ground black pepper
handful of baby salad leaves, to serve

Stir the lemon zest into the softened butter.

Roll the bread slices out with a rolling pin until thin, then spread each one with an even layer of lemon butter. Top with a thin layer of smoked salmon and season with black pepper.

Roll each slice up into a long sausage. Wrap in cling film (plastic wrap) and chill in the refrigerator for at least 15 minutes until set, or for up to 4 hours.

Unwrap the rolls and, using a sharp knife, cut each one crossways into 10 bite-sized pinwheels.

Arrange on a platter or a wooden board with some baby salad leaves to garnish.

WINNER. Artichoke hearts are an essential storecupboard ingredient for me. This recipe is one of my favourites – delicious, quick and simple to make, it is inspired by my mother. I always serve this at Christmastime, with toasted rosemary focaccia. It is rich, comforting, and everyone always wants the recipe.

HOT ARTICHOKE DIP

Serves 8

1 x 400 g (14 oz) tin artichoke hearts
   in water, drained
100 g (3½ oz/generous ⅓ cup) mayonnaise
100 g (3½ oz/1½cups) grated Parmesan

Preheat the oven to 200°C (180°C fan/400°F/
Gas 6).

Place all the ingredients in a food processor
and blend together.

Transfer the mixture to an ovenproof dish and
bake for 10–15 minutes until golden brown.

Dried orange garlands

THIS IS the most wonderful time for rituals and traditions: from decorating the tree, hanging the lights and making a wreath for my door. It is always a simple rustic feel for me with festive foliage and handmade decorations of sorts, including dried orange garlands, orange pomanders (see page 98), stringing paper chains together and unwrapping my favourite decorations from the box. A room full of Christmas songs, is where I always feel a sense of happiness and nostalgia. Homemade presents are often the best, from biscotti to jams to potting hellabores, and writing cards – I love to get lost in it all. Merry Christmas, E x

Festive and pretty – these dried orange slices can be hung as a garland or, if you are feeling very creative, sewn into a wreath. Christmas music is essential while making these, with a mug of mulled wine, I think.

You will need: 2–3 plump oranges (depending on how many you want to make) and festive string.

Preheat the oven to its lowest possible temperature.

Slice the oranges thinly, place onto some kitchen paper and pat dry. Now, place the orange slices in a single layer onto a baking sheet lined with baking parchment.

Bake for 3–4 hours, turning them over
halfway through. Remove and leave
to cool overnight.

The next day, thread with string for
a gorgeous homemade decoration.

CHRISTMAS GLAZED HAM WITH CLEMENTINES AND CLOVES

Serves 8

5–6 kg (11–13 lb) good-quality ham, ideally on the bone
10 black peppercorns
4 bay leaves
2 celery sticks with leaves, chopped
1 onion, chopped
4 carrots, roughly chopped
20 cloves

For the glaze
2 tablespoons Dijon mustard
3 tablespoons soft brown sugar
150 ml (5 fl oz/scant ⅔ cup) orange juice
zest of 1 clementine
squeeze of ketchup

To serve
Dijon mustard
Flat-leaf Parsley Sauce (see page 95)

Place the ham into a very large pot and add the peppercorns, bay leaves and chopped vegetables. Pour over enough water to cover the ham and cover with a lid. Bring to the boil, then immediately reduce the heat to low. Simmer gently for 3½ hours, topping up with water as necessary.

When the ham is cooked, the meat will be firm. Remove the pot from the heat and leave to cool.

Meanwhile, preheat the oven to 180°C (160°C fan/350°F/ Gas 4).

For the glaze, mix together the mustard, sugar, orange juice, clementine zest and ketchup in a bowl.

Drain the cooled ham of its cooking liquor and remove the skin, leaving as much fat on as possible. Evenly score the fat all over using the tip of a sharp knife and stud each diamond shape with a clove. Place the ham in a roasting tin (pan).

Using a pastry brush, brush half of the glaze evenly all over the ham. Roast in the oven for 10 minutes, then remove and brush the rest of the glaze on top. Return to the oven for a further 20 minutes, or until the glaze is sticky, golden brown and slightly set.

Serve with mustard and parsley sauce.

SMALL WONDERS. Christmas flavours. My glazed ham recipe will brighten up your table over the festive time. I like to keep Christmas as simple as possible and getting ahead in the kitchen is always one of the parts I enjoy the most. The anticipation of the days ahead, the excitement of planning the menu. Thinly sliced, this also makes the best ham sandwich ever.

PARSLEY SAUCE and glazed ham? Yes, please! For me, parsley sauce is the sauce of dreams – a classic combination that is simply delicious. Flat-leaf parsley is robust and stands up to the rich white sauce.

FLAT-LEAF PARSLEY SAUCE

Serves 8

30 g (1 oz) unsalted butter
30 g (1 oz/¼ cup) plain (all-purpose) flour
600 ml (20 fl oz/2½ cups) milk
8 tablespoons finely chopped flat-leaf parsley
Cornish sea salt and freshly ground black pepper

Melt the butter in a saucepan over a medium heat. Stir in the flour with a wooden spoon to make a roux and cook for 1–2 minutes. Remove the pan from the heat and use a small whisk to gradually stir in the milk to get a smooth sauce.

Return the pan to the heat and bring to the boil, stirring all the time. Simmer gently for 8–10 minutes, then season with salt and pepper.

Stir in the parsley and serve immediately.

LIFE IS SWEET. Chewy, sweet and delicious, meringue is loved by all. This is a wonderful pudding that works with different seasonal fruits – so, for me, it fits into many different times of the year. This recipe, with passsion fruit and clementine curd, has flavours of Christmas and will chase any winter blues away. Passion fruit are perfumed and full of flavour – they are generally sold when they are smooth to the touch, but are not truly ripe until they are lightly pitted, wrinkled and gnarly, which indicates they are juicy. Passion fruit always feel jewel-like to me and are a must at Christmastime.

MERINGUE ROULADE WITH CLEMENTINE CURD, CREAM AND PASSION FRUIT

Serves 12

For the clementine curd
finely grated zest and juice of 4 clementines
40 g (1¾ oz/3 heaped tablespoons) caster
    (superfine) sugar
2 large eggs
50 g (2 oz) unsalted butter, cut into cubes

For the meringue
6 egg whites
350 g (12 oz/1½ cups) caster (superfine) sugar
icing (confectioner's) sugar, for dusting

To decorate
300 ml (10 fl oz/1¼ cups) double (heavy) cream
6 ripe passion fruit, halved
a few fresh rosemary sprigs

Start by making the clementine curd. Bring a small pan of water to a simmer. Meanwhile, put the clementine zest and juice, sugar and eggs into a heatproof bowl and whisk together. Add the cubed butter and set the bowl over the pan of simmering water. Whisk for about 10 minutes until the curd thickens. Set aside.

Preheat the oven to 200°C (180°C fan/400°F/Gas 6). Line a shallow-lipped, 36 x 30 cm (14 x 12 in) baking tray (pan) with baking parchment, ensuring it comes up the sides.

For the meringue, put the egg whites into a large grease-free mixing bowl and whisk to stiff peaks, then slowly add the caster sugar until combined. Do not overmix.

continued...

Spread the meringue mixture evenly over the prepared baking tray and bake for 10 minutes, then reduce the oven to its lowest temperature and continue to bake for a further 15 minutes.

Remove the meringue from the oven and allow to cool slightly. Place a piece of baking parchment on the work surface, dust lightly with icing sugar, then confidently turn the roulade out onto the paper, crust-side down. Carefully peel away the lining paper and allow to cool.

When you are ready to roll, spread the clementine curd over the surface of the meringue. Whip the cream until to soft peaks and spread it over the curd. Spread the juice and seeds of the passion fruit over the cream. Take one short end of the baking parchment and use it to help roll up the roulade.

Place the finished roulade on a white serving plate, dust with more icing sugar, and decorate with rosemary sprigs.

ORANGE CLOVE POMANDERS

These oranges are simply pierced with cloves. As the fruit dries, it releases the fragrance of Christmas. Tie with ribbon for a festive look. You will need: a few oranges (depending on how many you want to make), festive ribbon or string, drawing pins and a handful of cloves.

Select a plump, round orange. Wrap a festive ribbon or string around the circumference, twist it tightly at the bottom and secure – a drawing pin works well for this. Bring the ends of the ribbon back up and around the orange, at a 90-degree angle to form a cross shape, and tie a knot. Tie the ends of the ribbon together to create a hanging loop.

Push cloves into the skin all around the orange. I like to completely fill the orange with cloves. Breathe in the fragrance. Place in a cool room for a few days to allow to dry. When dry, hang from the Christmas tree or place in a bowl in the hallway or as a table centrepiece. The aroma will last for days.

SPRING
TIDES

SPRING TIDES (HAVING A YARN)

DEAR SPRING. As winter finally wanes, I am
ready for you. Finally, spring is here and it is time
to look up. Warm, not with sunshine yet, but with
an air of romance, hope and, with blossom in
abundance on the trees, a promise of things to
come. Listen to the world and all it has on offer.
Each day begins with layers of birdsong; the
sounds of nature. Everyone seems happier and
walks with purpose and a smile. Nodding, you'll
hear the Cornish twang of 'Alright?', 'Yeh, you?'
or the common expression 'Will do'.

I love this season as the earth slowly wakes up
from the long Cornish winter. It's a time for so
many wonderful ingredients to fill your kitchen
with and be inspired to cook. Wellies on, I head
outside to forage. Sea beets appear, as do
wild primroses. Wild garlic is often found on a
woodland walk – green vibrant leaves and pretty
white flowers with a subtle, wonderful fragrance.
The call comes in that asparagus is ready to pick;
the green shoots growing above the sandy soil,
with salt blown in off the sea lands among the
spears, improving their flavour.

The windy open moors covered in bright yellow gorse are very much part of the beautiful wild landscape of Cornwall. Gorse has delicious coconut-scented flowers and I sometimes use them to infuse with my panna cotta recipe (see page 196). In late spring, sea pinks appear on the coast, framing the cliff edges, and the seaside hedgerows never disappoint – the Alexanders are always such a joyful sight when they return and their flowers in shades of yellow and green start reaching for the sky.

Days are lighter now, which gives me new energy to be creative. When not in my kitchen, I am usually found on the beach, watching the wonder of the wildlife, listening to the noise of the sea, comforted by familiar surroundings and not for one minute taking it for granted. Breakfast tea in my flask, blanket under my arm – I was always old before my time.

Spring is the world's favourite season – nature's showcase that all things are possible. On wings of hope the starlings arrive from their long journey, blossom blooms, a sea of bluebells appear. I enjoy the abundance before the mellow, golden summer arrives.

CORNISH CRAB – from crab cakes to crab sandwiches, nothings says Cornwall more to me. This recipe would perhaps be a last meal request for me – it contains all the ingredients that I simply love. Crab, pasta, lemon, parsley, chilli, Parmesan and olive oil… the textures and flavours of pure happiness. Crab is available in most good supermarkets or, even better, head to your local fishmonger. If on holiday in Cornwall, find a local fisherman to point you in the right direction. Just Shellfish in Port Isaac is my first point of call.

CORNISH CRAB LINGUINE WITH CHILLI, LEMON AND PARSLEY

Serves 4

300 g (10½ oz) dried linguine pasta
250 g (9 oz) fresh white Cornish crab meat,
    picked over for pieces of shell
2 fresh red chillies, deseeded and finely chopped
1 bunch of flat-leaf parsley, roughly chopped
zest and juice of 1 lemon (zest is optional)
100 g (3½ oz) Parmesan, grated
150 ml (5 fl oz/scant ⅔ cup) olive oil, for drizzling
Cornish sea salt and freshly ground black pepper

Bring a pan of salted water to the boil, add the pasta and cook according to the packet instructions.

Meanwhile, combine the crab meat in a large bowl with the chilli, parsley, lemon juice and zest, if using. Stir together.

Drain the pasta (reserve some of the cooking water) and add to the crab sauce along with a couple of tablespoons of the pasta cooking water. Use tongs to thoroughly mix the pasta with the crab so that all the pasta gets a good coating of sauce.

Serve in warmed bowls and sprinkle over a generous amount of Parmesan, a drizzle of olive oil and a grinding of black pepper. It goes deliciously with a cold glass of sauvignon blanc.

MEMORIES of teatime or breakfast at home as a child, with a sprinkling of sugar or a dollop of ketchup. Whenever my children have asked, 'What's for tea?', eggy bread is always a loved answer to that question. Sourdough is simply dipped in egg, then pan-fried in butter until golden brown. It can then be dusted with icing (confectioner's) sugar for a sweet treat or is moreishly good with crispy smoked bacon.

EGGY BREAD

Serves 4

4 large free-range eggs
3 tablespoons milk
4 slices of sourdough bread
1 tablespoon olive oil
2 tablespoons butter
Cornish sea salt and freshly
    ground black pepper

Crack the eggs into a large bowl, then add the milk and a pinch each of sea salt and black pepper. Whisk together with a fork.

Heat a frying pan (skillet) over a medium heat. Dip the slices of bread, one at a time, into the egg mixture, making sure they are well coated. Add half of the olive oil to the pan along with half of the butter and carefully move it around until melted. Remove the bread from the egg mixture and allow the excess to drip off, then carefully lower into the hot pan. Cook for 4–5 minutes until golden brown, then flip over using a spatula and cook the other side.

Remove and set aside while you cook the other slices.

WILD about wild garlic. An esssential springtime ingredient, from mid-March until early May, foraged wild garlic with its subtle fragrance is lovely to use in so many dishes. When it is in season, like asparagus, I try to use it as much as possible in my kitchen. It works in pesto, risottos, pasta, scones, in warm salads, and I particularly like it with soft scrambled eggs. Spinach is a perfect replacement if you are unable to find wild garlic. Like spinach, it shrinks on wilting, so you always need more than you think.

SCRAMBLED EGGS, WILTED WILD GARLIC, SOURDOUGH TOAST

Serves 4

200 g (7 oz) wild garlic
1–2 tablespoons unsalted butter, plus extra to serve
drizzle of olive oil
4 eggs
Cornish sea salt and freshly ground black pepper
toasted sourdough bread, to serve

Wash the wild garlic and trim off any tough ends.

Heat a frying pan (skillet) over a medium heat with a knob of butter and a drizzle of oil. Once hot, add the wild garlic with a pinch of salt and leave to wilt – this will take only a minute. Remove from the heat and set aside.

Whisk the eggs in a bowl and add a pinch of sea salt. In a separate pan, gently heat another knob of butter. Pour in the eggs, stirring continuously. Cook for a couple of minutes, then remove from the heat and let the eggs carry on cooking in the pan.

Serve the eggs and wilted wild garlic on buttered toast with unsalted butter and a cup of tea.

Crib time in Cornwall – this denotes time to stop for a mid-morning or afternoon snack, when you can drink tea, eat cake or reach for a pasty. It is an essential part of the way of life here and is never missed.

SPRING UP. Delicious new season lamb. I often cook this dish at the St. Tudy Inn for Sunday lunch. I prepare the lamb with the garlic, paprika and thyme the night before – this marinates the lamb, which gives it a delicious flavour. I prefer to use lamb shoulder as it has more fat, which again adds to that all-important flavour, but a leg of lamb also works well. To accompany it, redcurrant jelly or mint sauce are classics; in the autumn, I make a damson jam to serve with it, as we are lucky enough to have a damson tree that grows wild and beautiful.

SLOW-ROASTED LAMB SHOULDER WITH SMOKED PAPRIKA, GARLIC AND THYME

Serves 6–8

1 whole garlic bulb
100 g (3½ oz) fresh thyme, leaves picked
   with a few sprigs left whole
2 tablespoons smoked paprika
4 tablespoons olive oil
50 g (2 oz) unsalted butter
2.25 kg (5 lb 8 oz) whole shoulder of lamb, skin on
1 lemon, halved
250 ml (8½ fl oz/1 cup) water
Cornish sea salt and freshly ground black pepper
steamed tenderstem broccoli spears, to serve

Preheat the oven to 160°C (140°C fan/320°F/Gas 2).

Peel half of the garlic cloves, then lightly crush them in a pestle and mortar with some sea salt. Mix in the thyme leaves and paprika. Gradually add the oil, grinding until you have a thick paste.

Melt the butter in a small pan and stir it into the spice paste.

Put the lamb into a deep-sided roasting tin (pan) and rub it all over with the spice paste, then season with sea salt and black pepper. Add the whole sprigs of thyme, the remaining garlic cloves still in their skins and place the lemon halves in beside the lamb.

Cook, uncovered, in the oven for 35 minutes. Remove from the oven, pour in the water and use a ladle to baste the lamb all over with the water and cooking juices. Cover the lamb with foil and return it to the oven to roast for a further 3 hours, basting the meat every hour. For the last 15 minutes of cooking time, remove the foil. If the juices are evaporating rapidly, then add a little more water.

Remove from the oven, cover in foil and allow to rest for at least 15 minutes before slicing. Serve with the broccoli spears.

EFFORTLESS. My storecupboard recipe that I always reach for when in need of a quick lunch or supper. Deliciously simple and always a crowd pleaser, it's essential to have a glass of red on the go when cooking this.

WEEKEND SPAGHETTI WITH GARLIC AND CHILLI

Serves 4

350 g (12 oz) spaghetti
90 ml (3 fl oz/6 tablespoons) olive oil, plus extra to serve
4 garlic cloves, finely chopped
2 red chillies, finely chopped
sea salt and freshly ground black pepper

Bring a large saucepan of salted water to the boil and throw in the pasta. Stir and cook for 10–12 minutes or according to the packet instructions.

Meanwhile, gently heat the olive oil in a frying pan (skillet), add the garlic and chilli, and cook just until the garlic starts to brown (do not burn, otherwise it will be bitter).

Drain the pasta reserving a little of the cooking water. Add to the frying pan along with a couple of tablespoons of the reserved water. Season, stir through and serve with extra olive oil.

PLUMP, sweet scallops. I love nothing more than simply pan-frying them with herbs and butter, and serving them back in their shells seems a natural thing to do. Scallops can be a delicate starter or a heartier main course with home-cut fries and a bottle of chilled Gruner-Veltliner. Simple pleasures.

HAND-DIVED CORNISH SCALLOPS, PAN-FRIED WITH THYME, GARLIC AND BUTTER

Serves 4

4 teaspoons olive oil
12 scallops, on the half shell (I remove the roes but,
    if you prefer, you can leave them on)
30 g (1 oz) unsalted butter
1 garlic clove, finely sliced
4 teaspoons picked thyme leaves
squeeze of lemon juice

Heat a medium frying pan (skillet) over a high heat, add the oil, then add the scallops and cook for 30 seconds on each side.

Add the butter, garlic and most of the thyme and cook for a further 1 minute. Add a squeeze of lemon juice and put the scallops back in their shells.

Spoon the pan sauce over the scallops and garnish with the remaining thyme leaves.

GREEN BEAUTIES. A pretty salad always dazzles. Artichokes, the most beautiful member of the thistle family. This salad is comforting and wonderful, singing with asparagus and notes of citrus, with soft, creamy quail eggs tucked into the leaves. Carta di musica *(music paper bread – so therapeutic to make and lovely with cheese – you can also buy it ready-made in Italian delis) adds a delicious crunch. It is worth sourcing some lovely salad leaves and edible flowers for this pretty starter. It really is beautiful, elegant, considered and delicious.*

SALAD OF BABY ARTICHOKES, ASPARAGUS, LEAVES AND QUAIL EGGS WITH LEMON DRESSING AND CARTA DI MUSICA

Serves 4

4 baby artichokes
1 lemon, halved
12 quail eggs
16 medium asparagus spears
200 g (7 oz) fresh salad leaves (chervil, chickweed, amaranth, rocket/arugula, or any baby mixed leaves or edible flowers of choice)
Cornish sea salt and freshly ground black pepper

For the *carta di musica*
150 ml (5 fl oz/scant ⅔ cup) water
150 g (5 oz/generous 1 cup) '00' flour
100 g (3½ oz/generous ¾ cup) semolina
good olive oil (ideally infused with a rosemary sprig), for brushing
fine Cornish sea salt

For the lemon dressing
200 ml (7 fl oz/scant 1 cup) good olive oil
zest of 2 lemons

Start with the *carta di musica*. Preheat the oven to 200°C (180°C fan/400°F/Gas 6).

In a large bowl, combine the water, flour and semolina with a pinch of salt. Bring together gently and knead into a dough. Divide the dough into 8 pieces and use a pasta machine to roll the dough out into 8 thin, rectangular sheets about 1 mm (1/16 in) thick.

continued...

Place on a baking sheet and bake in the oven for 5–6 minutes until golden and crisp. Brush with oil and season with sea salt.

For the lemon dressing, warm the olive oil in a pan, then add the lemon zest to the oil to infuse. Remove from the heat and let cool.

To make the salad, pull the outer leaves from the artichokes until the paler, softer leaves are seen. Cut the leaves across the tops, trim the ends of the stalks and use a vegetable peeler to pare back the stalks, keeping them similar sizes. Cut the artichokes into quarters and rub with the lemon halves, then drop them into a bowl of water acidulated with a squeeze of the lemon juice.

Bring a large saucepan of water to the boil, add the quail eggs and boil for 1 minute, then remove with a slotted spoon to a bowl of iced water.

Add the artichoke pieces to the still-boiling water and cook for 5 minutes until tender. Remove with a slotted spoon and refresh in iced water, then drain well once again.

Cut the tough ends of the asparagus spears off at a diagonal, add to the pan of still-boiling water and cook for 2 minutes. Drain and refresh in iced water.

Toss the artichokes, asparagus and salad leaves together, then season with the lemon dressing and some sea salt and black pepper, to taste. Arrange attractively on 4 serving plates, carefully looking at the textures, shapes and colours.

Carefully peel the quail eggs. Tuck them into the salads leaves, allowing 3 on each plate.

Drizzle with some more lemon dressing and place a shard of *carta di musica* on top of each salad.

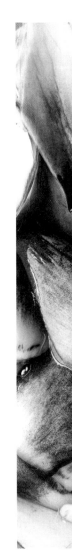

TOP BIRDS. Nothing is better than a comforting roast chicken with flavours of thyme, lemon, garlic and sea salt – an explosion of flavours that will bring deliciousness to your table. This is a meal that evokes memories of being together. I grew up with roast chicken, mash and peas – always peas. My mother would dry the wishbone on the Aga and I would close my eyes and make a wish with all my might. My family have always loved this, too. It's the meal that brings us together with great anticipation and makes us feel good.

SPRING ROAST CHICKEN WITH WILD GARLIC, HERBS, ROAST NEW POTATOES AND TARRAGON MAYO

Serves 4

1 medium free-range chicken
a few sprigs of fresh thyme, leaves picked
100 g (3½ oz) unsalted butter, softened
   (keep the paper the butter is wrapped in)
olive oil, for drizzling
1 lemon, halved
4 garlic cloves, unpeeled
a handful of wild garlic (foraged)
Cornish sea salt and freshly ground black pepper
Tarragon Mayo (see page 43), and Roast New Potatoes
   with Thyme and Garlic (see page 42), to serve

Preheat the oven to 200°C (180°C fan/400°F/Gas 6).

Wash and pat the chicken dry, then season with sea salt and black pepper. Mix the thyme and butter together. Ease the chicken skin away from the breasts with your hands to make a pocket and stuff with half of the thyme butter, easing it under the skin. Rub the ouside of the skin with the remaining thyme butter and a splash of olive oil. Season the skin with sea salt and black pepper. Push the two lemon halves into the cavity along with the garlic cloves and the wild garlic leaves (reserve the wild garlic flowers for decoration). Use the butter wrapper (or a piece of baking parchment) to cover the breasts for the first part of cooking.

Place the chicken in a roasting tin (pan) and roast in the oven for 30 minutes. Remove the butter paper and baste the chicken with its juices, then return to the oven to roast for a further 1 hour.

Remove from the oven and set aside to rest for 15–20 minutes. Serving with a side of tarragon mayo and roasted new potatoes.

REAL GEMS. They're sweet, crunchy and a beautiful shape, and I like to use them in salads. Wilting lettuce down shows its beautiful shape and brings out bittersweet notes – a wonderful way of eating lettuce in a slightly different way. Keen's Cheddar is rich and dense with layers of flavour. If you can't find it, a medium to strong Cheddar will work well in this recipe.

LITTLE GEM TART WITH KEEN'S CHEDDAR, SPRING ONIONS AND FLAT-LEAF PARSLEY

Serves 8

olive oil, for shallow frying and brushing
bunch of spring onions (scallions), finely sliced
1 x 375 g (13 oz) ready-rolled puff pastry sheet
200 g (7 oz) Keen's Cheddar (or any good-quality
　strong Cheddar), grated
2–3 Little Gem lettuce
2 tablespoons chopped flat-leaf parsley
Cornish sea salt and freshly ground black pepper

Preheat the oven to 200°C (180°C fan/400°F/Gas 6).

Heat a little olive oil in a frying pan (skillet) over a medium heat, add the spring onions and a splash of water and cover the pan with a lid so they steam for a few minutes. Remove the lid and continue to cook until tender and turning golden. Remove from the heat and let cool.

Unroll the puff pastry on its paper onto a baking sheet and score a 5mm (¼ in) border around the edge using the tip of a sharp knife. Make patterns around the border, if you like. Add the grated Cheddar to the spring onions, season well and tip everything onto the pastry, spreading it out to the border.

Cut the lettuce into quarters. In a bowl, mix the chopped parsley with a little olive oil and plenty of seasoning and brush the mixture all over the lettuce. Fry in the same pan you used for the spring onions until the lettuce just starts to turn golden at the edges.

Arrange the lettuce on the tart and bake in the oven for 10 minutes, or until the pastry is puffed and starting to brown. This is best served straight from the oven.

NOURISHING and restorative – all you will ever need is a second helping. Delicious come rain or shine, well or unwell, this will make you feel good. It's also a perfect way of using up any leftover chicken from your roast lunch or supper. Marnie, my grandmother, always made her chicken soup for us. It felt like a treat, as did being offered a fizzy drink from the SodaStream.

MARNIE'S CHICKEN SOUP WITH WILD GARLIC, SPINACH AND SPRING HERBS

Serves 6

For the stock
2 onions, roughly chopped
2 carrots, roughly chopped
2 celery stalks, roughly chopped
2 fresh bay leaves
bunch of fresh thyme
4 whole peppercorns
pinch of Cornish sea salt
1 x roasted free-range chicken carcass,
    with leftover meat still attached

For the soup
knob of unsalted butter
1 tablespoon olive oil
2 garlic cloves, finely sliced
4 shallots, finely sliced
handful of flat-leaf parsley, leaves and stalks
    separated and finely chopped
4 carrots, thinly sliced
4 celery stalks, plus leaves, thinly sliced
200 g (7 oz) wild garlic, leaves shredded,
large handful leafy spinach leaves or cavolo nero, tinned
    sweetcorn (corn) (optional, but delicious to add)
1 tablespoon lemon juice, or to taste

continued...

Start with the stock. Place the roughly chopped onions, carrots and celery in a large pan with the bay leaves, thyme, peppercorns, sea salt and the chicken carcass. Fill the pan with enough cold water so that everything is covered and bring to the boil. Reduce to a simmer and cook for 1 hour, skimming off any scum that rises to the surface from time to time.

About 15 minutes before the stock is ready, start the base of the soup. Heat the butter and olive oil in another large pan over a low heat. Add the garlic, shallots and parsley stalks and cook for 5–10 minutes, or until the shallots are translucent and soft. Add the carrots and celery and cook for a further 5 minutes.

When the stock is ready, remove the chicken carcass, pull off any remaining pieces of meat, shred and set aside, then discard the carcass. Strain the stock through a sieve into the vegetable pan, bring to the boil, then reduce the heat to low and simmer for 15 minutes. Add the shredded wild garlic and cook for a further 5 minutes. Add the spinach or cavolo nero. A drained tin of sweetcorn is also delicious and adds colour.

Finish the soup by squeezing in the lemon juice. Close your eyes and taste.

Divide the soup between serving bowls and top with the leftover shredded chicken, parsley leaves, wild garlic flowers and primrose flowers. Feel nourished.

GREEN. When asparagus is in season, we always eat it in abundance, as the season is so short. These beautiful spears hail the arrival of warmer, gentler days ahead.

ROASTED ASPARAGUS

Serves 4

16 asparagus spears
a drizzle of good-quality olive oil
Cornish sea salt and freshly ground black pepper
freshly squeezed lemon juice, to serve

Preheat the oven to 200°C (180°C fan/400°F/Gas 6).

Wash and trim off the hard ends from the asparagus, then arrange the spears on a baking sheet lined with baking parchment. Drizzle with good olive oil, sea salt and freshly ground black pepper. Bake for 10–15 minutes or until the spears are lightly browned and tender. Remove from the oven, squeeze over some lemon juice and serve immediately.

JAMMY FIGS. A way to enjoy figs throughout the year – this makes a deeply flavoured jam that definitely goes beyond breakfast. Spread on toasted sourdough, with feta and rocket (arugula) or with coppa ham and the last of the tomatoes. Delicious with roast lamb on a spring's day.

FIG JAM

Makes 1 x 500 ml (17 fl oz) jar

1 kg (2 lb 4 oz) ripe figs, halved lengthways
zest and juice of 1 lemon
500 g (1 lb 2 oz/2¼ cups) caster (superfine) sugar

Place the halved figs, lemon zest and juice in a heavy-based pan over a low heat and gently cook until the figs are soft and tender and look jammy.

Meanwhile, put the sugar into a baking dish and warm it through in a moderate oven for about 15 minutes until hot to the touch, but not beginning to melt.

Add the warmed sugar to the figs and gently cook, stirring frequently, for a further 45 minutes. Keep an eye on it – you don't want the jam to catch and burn. It is ready when a small teaspoonful of the mixture dropped into a saucerful of cold water sets rather than runs.

Allow to cool, then spoon into a sterilised jar (see page 208) and seal. Once opened, store in the refrigerator, where it will keep for up to 2 months.

CELEBRATE citrus. This posset is everything that a pudding should be: creamy, sweet, sharp, yet comforting. A simple and delicious recipe, and a perfect pudding for supper with friends, as you can dress it up or down. Lemons are one of the kitchen essentials that I would not be without. Like all citrus, it is a winter fruit, but to me they sing of summer and sunshiny days...

CITRUSY LEMON POSSET

Serves 8

800 ml (27 fl oz/scant 3¼ cups)
   double (heavy) cream
4 lemons: peeled rind of 3; juice of 4
250 g (9 oz/generous 1 cup) caster
   (superfine) sugar

To serve
1 punnet fresh raspberries
icing (confectioner's) sugar, for dusting

Place the cream, lemon rind and sugar in a pan and heat gently until the sugar has dissolved and the cream is steaming. Remove from the heat and allow to cool a little.

Pass the infused cream through a sieve (fine-mesh strainer) into a clean bowl to remove the rind. Stir in the lemon juice, then pour the posset mix into French bistro glasses. Place in the refrigerator to set.

When set, top with raspberries. I think a dusting of icing sugar over the berries slightly sweetens and, further, adds a pretty finish.

Note: Delicious served with a Cornish Fairing (see page 134).

NEEDED ALWAYS, my chocolate brownies. I use 54 per cent dark chocolate to make them, which adds a touch of luxury. Over the years, they are something I have found myself making as a treat or a pick-me-up. I never tire of them. The hazelnuts are optional – in my restaurant, I dress the brownies up with a touch of sea salt as a petit four.

CHOCOLATE AND HAZELNUT BROWNIES

Makes 12

250 g (9 oz) unsalted butter, plus extra for greasing
200 g (7 oz) dark chocolate (54 per cent cocoa solids)
6 eggs
340 g (11½ oz/generous 1¾ cups) light brown sugar
150 g (5 oz/1¼ cups) plain (all-purpose) flour, sifted
pinch of Cornish sea salt, plus extra for sprinkling
150 g (5 oz/generous 1 cup) roasted hazelnuts
icing (confectioner's) sugar, for dusting

Preheat the oven to 180°C (160°C fan/350°F/Gas 4). Lightly grease a 20 cm (8 in) square baking tin (pan) and line with baking parchment.

Melt the butter and chocolate together in a heatproof bowl set over a pan of barely simmering water (make sure the base of the bowl doesn't touch the water). When the mixture is melted and smooth, lift the bowl off the pan and let cool a little.

Use a stand mixer or electric beaters to beat the eggs and sugar together in a large bowl until just incorporated. Add the cooled chocolate mixture to the egg and sugar bowl and fold together using a large metal spoon. Sift over the flour, add a pinch of salt and fold together. Fold in the hazelnuts.

Scrape the mixture into the prepared tin, level and bake for 20–25 minutes or until there is still a slight wobble when you gently shake the tin. Gooey brownies – nothing more delicious.

Let cool completely in the tin before dusting with icing sugar and cutting into squares. I always refrigerate my brownies, as this allows them to set. If serving as a *petit four*, cut into smaller squares and sprinkle with sea salt.

SPICED ginger biscuit with a moreish crunch. Cornish fairings; a holiday in Cornwall would not be the same without them. These crunchy biscuits have been made popular by Furniss and I have added desiccated coconut to mine, which gives a little more texture to the biscuit. Eaten straight from the oven they are chewy and when cooled are perfect for dunking into a strong cup of tea.

CORNISH FAIRINGS

Makes 10–12

60 g (2 oz) butter, softened
125 g (4 oz/1 cup) plain (all-purpose) flour
50 g (2 oz/generous ½ cup) desiccated (dried shredded) coconut, plus extra for dusting
2 level teaspoons baking powder
1¾ level teaspoons bicarbonate of soda (baking soda)
1 tablespoon ground ginger
60 g (2 oz/generous ¼ cup) caster (superfine) sugar
75 g (2½ oz/3¾ tablespoons) golden (light corn) syrup

Preheat the oven to 150°C (130°C fan/300°F/Gas 1). Line a baking sheet with baking parchment.

Put the softened butter in a mixing bowl, then add all the dry ingredients except the sugar and mix together. Stir in the sugar and golden syrup.

Roll pieces of the mixture into 20 g (¾ oz) balls (about the size of a large grape) and place on the baking sheet. Make sure they are spaced well apart as they will spread out during cooking.

Bake in the oven for 10 minutes (you might need to do this in batches). Remove and let cool before eating.

Note: To make them into a crumb for sprinkling, allow to cool completely and whiz up in a blender.

SIMPLY AFFOGATO

Serves 2

6 scoops of vanilla-seeded ice cream
4 Almond and Pistachio Biscotti (see
 page 142)
2 shots of freshly made espresso

Scoop the ice cream into bowls and
crumble some biscotti over the top of the
ice cream. Decorate with a whole biscotti
on the side of each bowl.

Make the espressos and serve on the
side for drowning the ice cream in.

*SIMPLICITY. Creamy, delicious ice cream
drenched in espresso – such a simple
pudding that brings so much happiness
to me. My biscotti biscuits crumbled over
the top give it texture and a sweet, rich
nuttiness. A quick and easy pudding that
can be livened up with a shot of Frangelico
or two.*

CANDY PINK RHUBARB COMPOTE

Makes 500 g (1 lb 2 oz)

1 kg (2 lb 4 oz) rhubarb
zest and juice of 2 oranges
1 vanilla pod (bean), split lengthways
125 g (4 oz/generous ½ cup) caster
 (superfine) sugar

Preheat the oven to 120°C (100°C
fan/225°F/Gas ¼).

Wash the rhubarb and cut into uniformly
sized pieces and arrange in a baking dish.
Sprinkle the orange zest and juice over
the rhubarb and add the vanilla pod.
Sprinkle over the sugar.

Gently cook in the oven for 1 hour until
the rhubarb is tender but still holding its
shape. Allow to cool before serving.

*RHUBARB has arrived to brighten our days
and tide us over until a wider selection of
fruit becomes available. Rhubarb is actually
a vegetable, but its high acid content makes
it work better in sweet dishes rather than
savoury ones.*

WARMED and balanced by the addition of sugar and vanilla, rhubarb can be sharp, so, when cooking with it, it's important to taste as you go, and balance out that tartness. Early in the season, it is forced rhubarb that is available – pale and soft and more delicate in flavour.

Simply poached or lightly roasted, rhubarb is wonderful on porridge, with vanilla ice cream, panna cotta or here on sweet, crisp, yet chewy meringue. Clever eggs and sugar, delicious rhubarb, life is sweet.

PAVLOVA. Pure magic. There is something quintessentially English about this pudding. It evokes memories of warm, happy days, and is a pudding I have always loved making with my children. A show-stopping pavlova is a beautiful thing and wonderful to share with friends.

PAVLOVA WITH WHIPPED CREAM, POACHED RHUBARB AND PISTACHIOS

Serves 6

6 large egg whites
1 tablespoon white wine vinegar
1 tablespoon cornflour (cornstarch)
340 g (11½ oz/1½ cups) caster (superfine) sugar

To serve
300 ml (10 fl oz/1¼ cups) double
    (heavy) cream, whipped
1 x recipe quantity Candy Pink
    Rhubarb Compote (see page 136)
150 g (5 oz/1 cup) shelled pistachios,
    skins on, roasted and chopped

Preheat the oven to 130°C (110°C fan/250°F/Gas ¼). Line a baking sheet with baking parchment.

In a large mixing bowl, whisk the egg whites to stiff peaks. Add the white wine vinegar and cornflour, and whisk in. Gradually add the sugar very slowly while continuing to whisk, until the meringue is very stiff and shiny. To test if it ready, carefully turn the bowl over on top of your head – it should stay firmly in the bowl.

On your parchment-lined baking sheet, draw a circle around a 20 cm (8 in) cake tin, then turn the parchment over. Put a dab of meringue in each corner of the baking sheet to secure the parchment to the sheet. Spoon the meringue into the middle of the circle and spread it out to fill the drawn shape, leaving about a 1 cm (½ in) gap inside to allow the meringue to spread when cooking. Build up the sides of the meringue, leaving a dip in the middle for filling later.

Bake for 1 hour 15 minutes until the edges feel firm. Remove from the oven and leave to cool on the baking sheet.

Carefully transfer your meringue to a serving plate and fill with whipped cream, top with rhubarb compote, sprinkle with the pistachios, and eat.

MORNING café au lait companion, or teatime treat, biscotti are delicious to dunk and, of course, to crumble over ice cream.

ALMOND AND PISTACHIO BISCOTTI

Makes 24

110 g (3¾ oz/scant 1 cup) plain (all-purpose) flour,
    plus extra for dusting
1 teaspoon baking powder
50 g (2 oz/½ cup) ground almonds (almond meal)
25 g (1 oz/3 tablespoons) pistachios, roughly chopped
75 g (2½ oz/⅓ cup) caster (superfine) sugar
1 egg

Preheat the oven to 170°C (150°C fan/340°F/Gas 3). Line a baking sheet with baking parchment.

Sift the flour and baking powder into a large bowl. Add the ground almonds, pistachios and sugar and give it a good mix. Add the egg and mix it together, first with a wooden spoon and then using your hands to bring the mixture together to form a smooth dough.

Place the dough on a lightly floured surface and, using your hands, roll it into a log about 28 cm (11 in) long. Put it on the lined baking sheet and bake it on the middle shelf of the oven for 30 minutes. Transfer to a wire rack and leave until completely cold.

Reduce the oven temperature to 160°C (140°C fan/320°F/Gas 2).

Use a bread knife to cut the biscotti into slightly diagonal slices, about 1 cm (½ in) wide. Place them back on the lined baking sheet and bake for another 30 minutes until pale gold and crisp. Transfer them back to the wire rack to cool. When completely cold, store in an airtight container. They will keep for up to two weeks.

Lovely variations on this recipe include using chopped dried apricots or cranberries.

LATE SPRING. I always love seeing the creamy white elderflowers in the hedgerows at Harlyn Bay at this time of year. For me, the distinctive scent and flavour heralds the long-awaited arrival of late spring and summer days. Choose a sunny day, carefully cut the stalks with scissors and keep the flowers upright so that the pollen – the source of much of that unique flavour and fragrance – will not be lost. Trim as much stalk off as you can before use and check for bugs. Delicate and pretty and bathed in sunshine, this cordial is not just to drink but also the base for ice cream and fool.

HARLYN ELDERFLOWER CORDIAL

Makes 1.5 litres (50 fl oz/6¼ cups)

15 heads of elderflower
500 g (1 lb 2 oz/generous 2 cups) caster
   (superfine) sugar
4 tablespoons quality runny honey
1 litre (34 fl oz/4 cups) water
2 unwaxed lemons: both zested; 1 juiced;
   1 thinly sliced

Head outside in the sunshine and pick some elderflowers. Wash the elderflower heads well.

Place the sugar and honey in a large saucepan and cover with the water. Gently bring to the boil, stirring until all the sugar has dissolved, then remove from the heat. Finely grate in the lemon zest and add the elderflower heads, upside down, making sure the flowers are completely submerged. Squeeze in the juice from one of the lemons and add the lemon slices to the pan, too. Pop the lid on and set aside to infuse for 24 hours.

When you're ready to strain your cordial, line a fine sieve (strainer) with muslin (cheesecloth) over a large bowl. If you don't have muslin, you can use good-quality paper towels. Pour through the cordial and store in sterilised bottles (see page 208).

Note: Drink diluted with water or soda over ice, decorated with elderflowers and mint. This elderflower cordial will keep in the refrigerator for at least 3 months.

SUMMER
SEAS

SUMMER SEAS (GONE FISHING)

SUNSHINY days. I always enjoy being up with the first rays of the sun, or waking an hour earlier to see the sunrise. The start of a new day is so wonderful – the first light, the sea calling to a new dawn. Cherishing life's simple pleasures – bees, butterflies and sunflowers. Nurturing nature and chasing that summer light until the sun sets.

Sculling out in the dinghy, heading out to sea from Port Isaac harbour in search of mackerel, or hauling in the lobster pots for the day's catch. Rolling on the waters, warm sunshine on your face and the familiar sound of gulls soaring above. Foraging for and catching what I cook is such a joy. Mackerel, line-caught and cooked simply over a fire or under a grill with butter, lemon and parsley, is beyond delicious, with a raw spinach and nasturtium-flower salad, lemon zest and good olive oil.

I love to cook and eat outside, keeping things simple. A firepit on the beach, monkfish on rosemary skewers, scallops roasted in their shells, line-caught mackerel, and something sweet and delicious like pineapple drowned in rum roasted over the hot coals.

Golden hour, opportunities await. Discover where the silver sand meets the blue waters and the colourful fishing boats bob.

'It was June, and the world smelled of roses. The sunshine was like powdered gold over the grassy hillside.'

MAUD HART LOVELACE

NASTURTIUMS are great fun to grow. This year, I planted them from seed and have watched with delight as they have grown and flourished. Beautiful, round green leaves and then, as if by magic, a pop of colour from the orange and bright red flowers. I love making nasturtium butter with the flowers: 150 g (5 oz) softened unsalted butter and 50 g (2 oz) finely chopped nasturtium flowers, gently mixed together with a pinch of sea salt and black pepper and a squeeze of lemon. Roll in cling film (plastic wrap) and chill or put into a small bowl to serve with potatoes or chicken or fish.

PORT ISAAC MACKEREL WITH A RAW SALAD OF COURGETTES, CHILLI, NASTURTIUM FLOWERS AND ROCKET

Serves 4

1 courgette (zucchini), cut into ribbons
1 fresh red chilli, deseeded and finely chopped
2 lemons: zest and juice of 1; 1 thinly sliced
4 whole mackerel, gutted, cleaned and scaled
a few sprigs of rosemary
olive oil, for drizzling
100 g (3½ oz) rocket (arugula) leaves
6 nasturtium flowers
Cornish sea salt and freshly ground black pepper

Preheat the grill (broiler) to high.

Place the ribbons of courgette into a bowl, add the chopped chilli and lemon zest, season with sea salt, and set aside.

Season the cavity of each fish and fill with rosemary sprigs and lemon slices. Rub the skin with a little oil, salt and pepper. Grill (broil) for about 6 minutes on each side, turning occasionally, until the skin is crisp and charred and the flesh is opaque.

Add the rocket leaves to the courgette salad, drizzle with olive oil and a squeeze or two of lemon juice. Gently tear the nasturtiums through the salad and toss to combine.

Place the whole mackerel on a plate with the courgette salad.

This recipe can also be cooked outside on the barbecue or baked in the oven for 10 minutes at 180°C (160°C fan/350°F/Gas 4).

Beach firepit (our way)

ALWAYS seek the consent of the owner of the beach before setting a fire, or make sure that fires or barbecues are allowed. You will need a spade, a metal grill, charcoal, small logs, matches, tongs, some small sticks for kindling – and, of course, for marshmallows.

Dig a hole and gather some slate and stones to create a wall to contain the charcoal. Place the charcoal in the pit, add kindling and light the fire. Once it has got going, place the grill over the top. Allow 20–30 minutes for the fire to get really hot before you start cooking on the grill.

When the sun has set and you are ready to go home, put the fire out and make sure you dispose of everything responsibly. Keep tidy – take your rubbish home.

LOBSTERS in Cornwall we have some of the finest lobsters – the cold seas make them sweet, rich and plump. There is nothing better than lobsters cooked to order over coals. When this goes on my menu it does not last long.

PORT ISAAC LOBSTER OVER FIRE WITH FINES HERBES

Serves 2

1 live lobster, about 650 g (1 lb 7 oz)
125 g (4 oz) unsalted butter, softened
2 garlic cloves, crushed
1 tablespoon olive oil
zest and juice of 1 lemon
100 g (3½ oz) tarragon, roughly chopped
100 g (3½ oz) flat-leaf parsley, roughly chopped
100 g (3½ oz) chives, roughly chopped
Cornish sea salt and freshly ground
    black pepper, to taste
kitchen herbs and garden salad leaves, to serve

Preheat a barbecue or the grill (broiler) to high.

Place the lobster on a chopping board. Insert a large, sharp, heavy knife into the cross on the back of the head and cut down towards the tail, cutting it in half. Remove the stomach and the black intestinal tract that may run through the middle of the tail and discard. If you prefer, buy your lobsters already cooked and halved (justshellfish.co.uk).

In a small pan, melt the butter with the crushed garlic and add the olive oil, lemon zest, lemon juice and chopped herbs.

Brush the lobster flesh with the butter mixture, season with salt and pepper, then place under the grill, flesh-side up (if using a grill plate/pan or barbecue, place flesh-side down) and cook for 4–5 minutes. Baste the lobster with the butter mixture and keep basting from time to time until it is cooked through, about 5–6 minutes further.

Serve on a plate with kitchen herbs and garden leaves. Nothing is more delicious.

MONKFISH, or lotte in French, is known as the poor man's lobster. It is a delicious, robust and wonderful ingredient that I love to cook and eat. It works so well with bolder flavours, such as curries, or can be cooked over fire or even refined by serving as a ceviche. Here, the combination of monkfish, chorizo and sun blush tomatoes is delicious. Threading them on to rosemary skewers is pretty and adds a depth of flavour to the fish.

MONKFISH, CORNISH CHORIZO AND SUN BLUSH TOMATOES ON ROSEMARY SKEWERS

Serves 8

1 x 200 g (7 oz) jar sun blush tomatoes,
   drained, reserving the oil
1 medium chorizo, about 225 g (8 oz), cut into
   1 cm (½ in) rounds
650 g (1 lb 7 oz) monkfish fillet, cut into chunks
12 long rosemary sprigs, plus extra leaves
   for sprinkling
100 ml (3½ fl oz/scant ½ cup) olive oil
Cornish sea salt and freshly ground black pepper

To serve
handful of rocket (arugula) leaves
hot buttered Cornish new potatoes
mixed leaf salad with edible flowers

Preheat a barbecue or grill (broiler) to high.

Place the sun blush tomatoes in a large bowl and add the sliced chorizo. Using a skewer, pierce a hole through each piece of monkish, then toss in the bowl with the tomatoes and chorizo. Thread alternately onto rosemary skewers, allowing 3 pieces of each ingredient on each skewer.

Barbecue or grill (broil) the monkfish skewers on all sides, keeping them moving, for a total of 6 minutes, or until browned at the edges. Drizzle with with olive oil and sprinkle with salt, pepper and rosemary leaves.

Lay the grilled monkfish skewers on rocket leaves and serve with hot buttered Cornish new potatoes and a kitchen leaf salad with summer flowers.

FIRESIDE at Boat Bay (the local name for Onjohn Cove), with childlike excitement, we always find ourselves toasting marshmallows on the beach. As the sun sets over the sea, warmed from a sip or two of Pineau, the world feels like a very happy place to be.

TOASTED GIANT MARSHMALLOWS

Serves 4

1 large pack giant marshmallows

Light a campfire

Put a marshmallow or three on a stick and hold over the fire to toast, turning the stick until the outside of the marshmallows is golden brown and the inside is just starting to get squidgy.

Eat while watching the sun set.

LAZY DAYS, warm sunshine, the smell of the pine trees in the heart of Provence and the comforting routine we always had with Marnie and Papa. Mealtimes were always a highlight, planned around what was available that morning from the local market.

Long lunches were followed by a siesta to shelter from the heat of the sun, which we were always eager to take as Papa would throw French sweets onto our beds as a wake-up call. We never went to sleep, always keeping our eyes half open, hoping that the hour would go really quickly and we could be outside by the pool, searching for lizards or finding crickets. How I would love a siesta these days! I think perhaps they should be compulsory.

Here in Cornwall, life can often feel slower. Living off people's high days and holidays, sometimes the days and weeks merge together. Under warm, dappled skies, I want to eat lighter food with gentle flavours under leafy trees, or pack a picnic and go beachside by the sea.

COOL CUCUMBER SALAD WITH CRÈME FRAÎCHE AND DILL

Serves 6

2 large cucumbers or 3–4 medium or small
 cucumbers, peeled
1 teaspoon Cornish sea salt
100 g (3½ oz/½ cup) crème fraîche, or to taste
1 tablespoon apple cider vinegar
small bunch of fresh dill, finely chopped

Start by finely slicing the cucumbers, either by hand with a good knife, or carefully using a mandoline or a food processor with a slicing disc. Put the sliced cucumber into a colander, sprinkle with the salt and leave the colander over a bowl. The salt will bring some of the liquid out of the cucumber, which will also turn slightly darker in colour.

Drain well (using your hands to squeeze the cucumbers to release any excess juice) and transfer the cucumber to a fresh bowl. Stir through the crème fraîche, vinegar and dill (adding a little more crème fraîche if you prefer a creamier salad).

Chill the salad in the refrigerator for 20 minutes before serving. Simply delicious.

My Cornish table

EATING OUTSIDE is one of life's simple pleasures from the firsts of the spring sunshine, to balmy summer nights that feel like they go on forever and then the warm autumnal sunshine that is intense and wonderful as the days start slowly drawing in we still find ourselves on the beach and by the sea. Long lunches at Harlyn Beach House under the ash tree looking over the fields towards the sea and the 'old man' (Cataclus) – there's nothing better.

For me, laying a table is all about keeping a stripped-back and simple look and using the things that make your house a home. Mismatched cutlery, Cornish blue crockery, my favourite French bistro glasses, dish-towel napkins, flowers cut from the garden depending on the time of year. In the colder months, I will often fill jam jars with winter herbs: rosemary, sage and thyme. I am a perfectionist, although I am slowly learning that some of the best moments come out of the chaos of not overplanning – so try to relax and enjoy bringing your own style and energy to whatever you do.

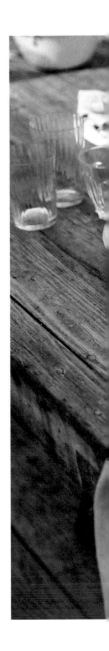

EN FAMILLE. *On summer days, my mother Lucy was always the best at bringing everyone together. This recipe of whole baked salmon is somewhat retro but it is a wonderful dish for the middle of a table, served alongside Cornish new potatoes with herbs and crème fraîche, bowls of garden leaves and wildflowers. Finish the meal with English strawberries, meringues and cream. Think of warm days, with Champagne by the glass, or chilled rosé. Days when life seems uncomplicated and simple.*

WHOLE BAKED SALMON WITH CUCUMBER, WATERCRESS AND MAYONNAISE FOR DAYS

Serves 8

100 ml (3½ fl oz/scant ½ cup) sunflower
   oil, for brushing
1 whole salmon, 2–3 kg (4–6 lb), gutted, cleaned and scaled
1 large sprig of flat-leaf parsley
2 lemons, cut into sunshine rounds
2 bay leaves
300 ml (10 fl oz/1¼ cups) white wine

To serve
thin cucumber slices
watercress
lemon rounds
Citrus Mayo (see Tarragon Mayo on page 43)

Preheat the oven to 200°C (180°C fan/400°F/Gas 6).

Take 2 large sheets of kitchen foil and place on top of each other in a roasting tin (pan). Brush oil over both pieces of foil, place the salmon on top of one of the foil pieces, then brush the salmon with oil, too.

Put the parsley, lemon slices and bay leaves into the body cavity. Crimp the edges of the foil together to make a parcel, but just before sealing, pour in the wine. Seal tightly and bake the fish in the oven for 50–60 minutes.

Allow the fish to cool in the parcel, then gently peel off the skin and serve cold, garnished with thinly sliced cucumber, watercress, lemon slices and citrus mayo.

Note: Leftover salmon can be used the next day in a salad with Cornish new potatoes, dill and mayo.

RED ALERT. A simple salad for warmer days, eating outside under the trees. Deliciously moreish and full of flavour, this can be a meal in itself but works equally well as an accompaniment. Evie has often taken it as a packed lunch to school.

RED CAMARGUE RICE WITH FETA AND SUMMER HERB SALAD

Serves 8

570 ml (19 fl oz/2⅓ cups) water
250 g (9 oz/1⅓ cups) red Camargue rice
2 shallots, peeled and finely chopped
3 spring onions (scallions), sliced
4 tablespoons chopped fresh mint
200 g (7 oz) rocket (arugula) leaves
200 g (7 oz) feta cheese
Cornish sea salt and freshly ground black pepper

For the dressing
1 garlic clove, crushed
½ teaspoon Cornish sea salt
1 teaspoon wholegrain mustard
1 tablespoon balsamic vinegar
2 tablespoons olive oil

In a large saucepan with a lid, bring the water to simmering point, add the rice and a pinch of sea salt, cover and gently cook for 40 minutes. Remove from the heat, keep the lid on and set aside for 15 minutes.

Make the dressing. In a small bowl, stir together the garlic, salt and mustard, then add the vinegar and whisk in the olive oil.

Pour the dressing over the rice, then add the shallots, spring onions, mint and rocket. Season to taste with salt and pepper and toss to combine. Just before serving, crumble over the feta cheese.

ROUNDS of oranges always make me think of sunshine. This salad is wonderful – I don't like raw onion in salads generally, but here I love the combination of the tangy orange, gentle raw fennel and sweet onion. It is joyous and can be eaten on its own or as a lovely accompaniment. In midwinter, blood oranges are a must and work just as beautifully.

ORANGE, RED ONION AND WATERCRESS SALAD

Serves 4

4 medium oranges
2 red onions
1 fennel bulb
200 g (7 oz) watercress
few sprigs of mint, finely sliced
juice of 1 lime
3 tablespoons olive oil
Cornish sea salt

Peel and slice the oranges crossways into rounds and try to save as much of the juice as possible for the dressing. Slice the red onions and fennel thinly.

Combine the onions and fennel with the orange slices and place on a serving plate with the watercress and sliced mint.

To make the dressing, combine the saved juice from the oranges with the lime juice and olive oil and season with salt. Drizzle over the salad and serve.

LOST BREAD and the glut of the last of the summer tomatoes, spring onions, herbs and olives. Yes, please! This is a bowl that sings summertime to me. Delicious on its own, it is also a perfect accompaniment to mackerel or bream.

A note on tomatoes: do not refrigerate them. Cold tomatoes lose all their flavour, so handle with care, if you can. Like everything, tomatoes are available throughout the year now, but do try to eat them in the summer when they are in season. There is nothing more delicious.

LAST OF THE SUMMER TOMATOES WITH TOASTED SOURDOUGH AND HIGH-NOTE HERBS

Serves 4

4 slices of day-old sourdough bread, broken into
    chunky croutons
800 g (1 lb 12 oz) tomatoes, at room temperature,
    chopped and deseeded
15 basil leaves, torn
1 small mixed bunch of tarragon, chives and
    parsley, chopped
350 g (12 oz) jar of stoned (pitted) black olives
    (or green, if you prefer), drained and halved
200 g (7 oz) spring onions (scallions), thinly sliced
120 ml (4 fl oz/½ cup) olive oil
Cornish sea salt and freshly ground black pepper

Preheat the oven to 170°C (150°C fan/340°F/Gas 3).

Spread the sourdough croutons over a baking sheet and bake in the hot oven until golden, 10–15 minutes. Leave to cook as you make the salad.

Place the chopped tomatoes in a large bowl, add all the other ingredients including the sourdough croutons, season with salt and pepper and toss together.

Leave to sit for 10 minutes before serving.

STRAWBERRIES seem to arrive earlier and earlier in markets and shops and can often be found all year round. I remember wonderful times as a child walking up the country lane from our house to our local strawberry farm, Coles, and picking our own. Returning with a trug of glossy red fruit, our chins and fingers stained red from the juice by the time we reached home.

Strawberries will only be found on my menu in the summer months here at the Inn. I could share so many recipes with you. Strawberries simply served with a bowl of crème fraîche, mint and Demerara sugar is one of my favourites – so simple but delicious. Or a classic old-fashioned sponge with whipped cream and halved strawberries. Jams, compotes, pavlovas, summer pudding, strawberry scones (jam first), a salad of strawberries, cucumber, mint and viola flowers...

SUMMERTIME and the living is easy. Summer light, warm sunshine and a gentle breeze surround me as I write this recipe underneath the shade of the cherry tree at home. Drawing inspiration from old family photos, I'm reminded of fond childhood memories of Neapolitan ice cream in a rectangular block, of 'strawberry feet' lollies and the classic Cornish Strawberry Mivvi.

This recipe using delicious, perfectly ripe strawberries is lovely and a good way to end a meal. If you are having a summer drinks party, this also makes a sweet canapé to wow your friends. If you are feeling more decadent, dip the freshly chocolate-coated strawberries into chopped pistachios or toasted coconut. At home, Evie likes to use sprinkles for a fun idea.

ENGLISH STRAWBERRIES DIPPED IN DARK CHOCOLATE

Serves 8

2 punnets of strawberries
250 g (9 oz) good-quality dark chocolate
   (54 per cent cocoa solids)

Wash and dry the strawberries. Line a baking sheet with baking parchment.

Melt the chocolate slowly in a heatproof bowl set over a pan of gently simmering water until smooth and shiny.

Dip the strawberries in the melted chocolate, then lay them on the prepared baking sheet. Allow them to rest, before eating, until the chocolate has set.

JELLY always brings a smile to my face. A childhood favourite, this strawberry, raspberry and orange jelly is wonderful. Lovely, light and palate cleansing, it's the perfect summer pudding.

SUMMER FRUIT JELLY WITH WHOLE ENGLISH STRAWBERRIES AND VANILLA ICE CREAM

Serves 8

300 g (10½ oz/3 cups) fresh strawberries,
 hulled and halved
125 g (4 oz/1 cup) fresh raspberries
60 g caster (superfine) sugar
150 ml (5 fl oz/scant ⅔ cup) water
300 ml (10 fl oz/1¼ cups) orange juice
4½ sheets of gelatine

To serve
150 g (5 oz/1½ cups) fresh strawberries, halved
vanilla ice cream

Place the strawberries and raspberries in a pan with the sugar, water and orange juice. Bring to the boil without stirring, then remove from the heat.

Place the gelatine in a bowl, cover with cold water and leave to soak for 5 minutes. Once softened, drain and squeeze out excess water from the gelatine. Place the gelatine back in the bowl and add a little of the warm fruit juices, stirring gently until the gelatine is completely dissolved. Pour into the fruit pan through a fine sieve (fine mesh strainer) and stir very gently.

Spoon the fruits into French bistro glasses and pour over the orange liquid from the fruit pan. Stir once more, then transfer to the refrigerator to set.

When set, decorate with halved strawberries and sprigs of mint. Serve with vanilla ice cream.

SUMMER FIGS. There are many varieties of figs. The delicate fruit can be eaten straight from the tree and slowly savoured (I always find myself closing my eyes as I take the first bite), made into jams or chutneys, or used in a tart, as in my recipe here. The beautiful leaves of the fig tree make perfect shade for the post-lunch siesta, which was always essential to escape the midday sun.

My fig tart is very simple to make and a wonderful pudding for the warmer months. Buttery layers of puff pastry and sweet jammy figs are simply baked in the oven, then topped with a dollop of crème fraîche and decorated with lavender flowers.

These tarts work equally well with ripe peaches or greengages, or try a savoury version with summer tomatoes. Any leftover puff pastry can be frozen or used to make Parmesan and Thyme Puff Pastry Twists (see page 46).

JAMMY FIG TART TOPPED WITH CRÈME FRAÎCHE AND LAVENDER FLOWERS

Serves 8

1 kg (2 lb 4 oz) ready-made puff pastry
plain (all-purpose) flour, for dusting
12 figs, halved lengthways
8 teaspoons granulated sugar
2 tablespoons redcurrant jelly

To serve
a dollop of crème fraîche, to serve
a few lavender flowers, for sprinkling

Preheat the oven to 200°C (180°C fan/400°F/Gas 6). Line 2 baking sheets with baking parchment.

Divide the pastry into 8 equal pieces, then thinly roll out each piece on a lightly floured surface and cut into 15 cm (6 in) circles. Place them onto the baking sheets, spaced well apart.

Cut each fig half crossways into slices and arrange them, slightly overlapping, on the pastry discs, leaving a 2.5 cm (1 in) border. Sprinkle each tart with a teaspoon of sugar and bake in the oven for 10–15 minutes until the pastry is puffed up and golden and the sugar has lightly caramelised.

Meanwhile, warm the redcurrant jelly in a small saucepan. When the tarts come out of the oven, lightly brush them with the redcurrant glaze. Serve with crème fraîche, sprinkled with lavender flowers.

HIGH
SUMMER

HIGH SUMMER (PICK YOUR OWN)

COLOURS of strawberries, raspberries, cherries, apricots, figs, currants, gooseberries and the first blackberries fill up my kitchen. There is so much inspiration to be found. Make sure you enjoy summer's finest ingredients while they are in season. I love heading to my local farm shop to pick my own strawberries. Golden and sweet apricots are a taste of the season and one of my favourite fruits. A peach is a perfect high-summer treat – essential, juicy, fleshy – I love nothing more than eating one with a baguette and some goat's cheese.

Warm sunshine, longer, lighter days, leafy trees, picnics, boat trips and days out. I think this time of year moves the world. It gives everyone more of a sense of adventure. I feel energised and excited. Arriving with my picnic packed at a patch of grass bathed in sunshine, I watch as the children investigate rock pools and scamper along the shoreline, building up their appetites. Summer salads with fragrant herbs and edible flowers are laid out alongside dishes of mackerel, grilled artichokes and heritage tomatoes; tubs filled with strawberries, raspberries, peaches and plump cherries. Perfect sunshine sustenance.

A way to tether summer down all year round is by preserving the best of the season's berries into jars. Simple strawberry jam, apricot and lavender jam, pickled cucumbers, fig chutney or blackcurrant compote – the choice is endless. My scaffold-board shelves are full of jars all in a row, with marmalades, compotes, jams and cordials of figs, cherries, Seville oranges, gooseberries and strawberries. It's just like finding treasure.

TIME. Enjoying our days in a whole new way. I love each season as it unfolds – breathe it in. It is in the simplicity of this dish that I find much of the pleasure. Mozzarella is the cheese that sings summertime to me. This makes a wonderful summer lunch to eat with sourdough, unsalted butter and some Cornish sea salt.

BUFFALO MOZZARELLA, BROAD BEAN, OLIVE, LEMON AND ROCKET SALAD

Serves 4

400 g (14 oz/3 cups) broad (fava) beans, podded, or peas
handful of black olives, pitted and halved
250 g (9 oz) rocket (arugula), washed
2 balls of buffalo mozzarella
zest of ½ lemon
Cornish sea salt and freshly ground black pepper

For the dressing
1 tablespoon Dijon mustard
1 tablespoon sherry vinegar
200 ml (7 fl oz/scant 1 cup) extra virgin olive oil
juice of ½ lemon
Cornish sea salt and freshly ground black pepper

Blanch the broad beans or peas in boiling water until tender. Drain and season, then place in a bowl along with the olives and the rocket and toss to combine.

Make the dressing. Put the mustard and sherry vinegar into a bowl and add a generous pinch of salt and pepper. Gradually add the olive oil, whisking to emulsify. Squeeze in the lemon juice and whisk to combine. Check the seasoning.

Tumble the salad onto a serving plate. Tear the mozzarella balls into 4 pieces and place on top. Drizzle with the dressing and scatter over the lemon zest.

PLANT UP. I am no gardener, but just after lockdown I decided, like many others, to try my hand at growing my own. Impatient by nature, I planted the seeds and wanted them to grow straightaway. Following the directions, I nurtured, watered, occasionally talked to and – with the help of the fine, sunny weather – triumphantly grew many things, including courgettes (zucchini). There will be no change in career for me – I will stick to cooking – but to dip my toe into gardening and to now own a wheelbarrow, well, that has made me very happy.

I love risotto. It's a dish we always eat at home and have on my restaurant menu. Ever popular, it's also a dish that you can eat throughout the year. There is something so wonderful about courgettes and their beautiful flowers, so very versatile, too. This lovely recipe is just delicious and something different, using up every part of the courgette and flower. It reminds me of long summer days, when supper is eaten outside and when the time seems endless. At this time of the year, sweet broad (fava) beans and peas are delicious and adding them to this risotto at the end just brings even more summery high notes.

COURGETTE-FLOWER RISOTTO

Serves 6

10 courgette (zucchini) flowers with baby
  courgettes still attached
2 tablespoons olive oil
1 garlic clove, finely chopped
1 small onion, finely chopped
400 g (14 oz/scant 2 cups) Carnaroli
  or Arborio risotto rice
1.5 litres (50 fl oz/6 cups) vegetable stock, hot
60 ml (2 fl oz/¼ cup) white wine
100 g (3½ oz) Parmesan, grated, or to taste
Cornish sea salt and freshly ground black pepper
fresh basil leaves, to serve

Detach the flowers from the courgettes, remove the stamens and gently wipe the flowers clean. Slice the courgettes into rounds.

Heat the olive oil in a large pan and fry the garlic and onion until softened. Add the courgette flowers and stir for 1 minute, then add the rice and stir until well coated in the oil. Pour over a ladleful of stock and stir until it is absorbed. Repeat until the stock is finished. Add the courgettes and stir through, then add the white wine. Cook for a further 5 minutes, then remove from the heat.

Add Parmesan and season with salt and pepper to taste. Serve garnished with basil leaves and extra Parmesan.

SIMPLE, yet never underestimate the humble carrot. I love the simplicity of this dish. Wonderful for a picnic or a quick lunch, it is delicious with walnut bread. In my restaurant I have served it as a starter and it always went down well, even with the most sceptical of guests.

To add another element, you can finely slice some fennel with a mandoline, if you have one, and mix together with the carrot, fronds and all.

SUMMER CARROT SALAD WITH FLAT-LEAF PARSLEY AND WHOLEGRAIN DRESSING

Serves 4

400 g (14 oz) carrots, grated
a bunch of flat-leaf parsley, roughly chopped

For the dressing
2 tablespoons white wine vinegar
3 tablespoons olive oil
2 tablespoons lemon juice
2 tablespoons wholegrain mustard
Cornish sea salt and freshly ground black pepper

Place the grated carrots and chopped parsley in a salad bowl.

Mix together all the ingredients for the dressing and season.

Pour the dressing over the salad and toss together. Taste and consider the seasoning.

SEASIDE LIVING. A wonderfully simple dish – try to source sustainable English prawns (shrimp). With chilli, olive oil, parsley and citrus notes of lemon, it makes a quick and easy lunch. Eat with abandon, preferably with a view of the sea.

ENGLISH TIGER PRAWNS, CHILLI, GOOD OLIVE OIL AND FLAT-LEAF PARSLEY

Serves 6

100 ml (3½ fl oz/scant ½ cup) good-quality olive oil
16 raw English tiger prawns (jumbo shrimp), in their shells
1 teaspoon chilli (red pepper) flakes
1 fresh red chilli, finely chopped
juice of 1 lemon, plus extra wedges to serve
handful of flat-leaf parsley, roughly chopped
Cornish sea salt
Citrus Mayo (see Tarragon Mayo, page 43), to serve

Heat the olive oil in a large frying pan (skillet) until it starts to sizzle. Add the prawns and chilli flakes and cook, shaking the pan from time to time, letting the prawns turn from their raw blue colour to golden pink. Turn the prawns over and add the fresh chilli, lemon and parsley. Season with sea salt.

Serve with citrus mayo and extra lemon.

FISH cookery is one of my favourite things. Keep it simple. John Dory is characterful and a joy to cook with. In this recipe I roast it quickly with just lemon, thyme and olive oil. Eat with a raw salad of baby spinach with lemon zest and a wholegrain mustard dressing. This recipe also works well with bass or bream. If you are unsure about preparing fish, always ask your fishmonger to gut and fillet the fish for you.

MR DORY, JOHN DORY SIMPLY ROASTED WITH LEMON AND THYME

Serves 2

2 medium or 4 small John Dory fillets
good olive oil, for drizzling
2 lemons (1 per person), sliced into sunshiny circles
fresh thyme leaves (lemon thyme is so fragrant)
Cornish sea salt and freshly ground black pepper

Preheat the oven to 220°C (200°C fan/430°F/Gas 8).

Wash and dry the fish, then place in a roasting tin (pan). Season each fillet on both sides with salt and pepper and drizzle generously with olive oil. Tuck the lemon slices and thyme leaves between the fish.

Roast in the oven for 10–12 minutes. Remove from the oven and spoon over the lemon-scented olive oil and cooking juices.

Note: Some warm sourdough bread to mop up the lemony, olive oily juices would be perfect.

WOBBLE. This recipe has been on my menu from the beginning; rich and creamy yet with a lightness to it that is unexpected. The perfect wobble is necessary and the vanilla seeds against the white background are so pretty. It is probably one of my most well-known recipes. I cooked it when I appeared on The Great British Menu *and Daniel Clifford said it was the best panna cotta he had ever tasted, scoring it 9/10 (that will do!). I have also shared here the recipes for my Blackberry Ice Cream and Cornish Fairings (see pages 239 and 134) that I served with it on the programme, so if you have a little more time, do make it a total lesson in simplicity.*

A wonderful pudding to eat on a warm summer's day. I actually cook this throughout the year, changing the fruit that it is paired with depending on the season: candy pink forced rhubarb in January, raspberries and English strawberries in the summer, but my favourite is blackcurrant compote. The panna cotta is so delicious, cool and soft that I think the sweet, sharp blackcurrants are the perfect accompaniment. Also, the deep, rich colour of the berries look so pretty against the creamy texture of the cooked vanilla cream.

VANILLA-SEEDED PANNA COTTA AND BLACKCURRANT COMPOTE WITH BROWN SUGAR SHORTBREAD

Serves 6

800 ml (26½ fl oz/3⅓ cups) double (heavy) cream
150 ml (5 fl oz/scant ⅔ cup) semi-skimmed
    (half-fat) milk
1 vanilla pod (bean), split
3 sheets of gelatine
150 g (5 oz/1¼ cups) icing (confectioner's)
    sugar, sifted

For the blackcurrant compote
300 g (10½ oz) blackcurrants, picked over
    and removed from the stems
200 g (7 oz/scant 1 cup) caster (superfine) sugar

To serve
Brown Sugar Shortbread Stars (see page 39)

First make the compote. Wash the blackcurrants in cool water and place in a saucepan. Add the sugar and bring to the boil over a medium heat, then reduce the heat and simmer for about 5 minutes, or until the blackcurrants have softened and split. Transfer to a bowl and allow to cool completely before chilling in the refrigerator.

For the panna cotta, pour half of the cream, all of the milk and the split vanilla pod (bean) into a heavy-based pan and slowly bring to a simmer. Once simmering, remove from the heat and leave to infuse for 10 minutes.

Immerse the gelatine in a small bowl of cold water and leave to soak.

In a separate bowl, combine the remaining cream with the icing sugar.

Return the infused cream mixture to the heat to warm through. Remove the gelatine from the water, squeezing out any excess liquid, then add to the warmed cream and stir to dissolve.

Pour the infused mixture through a fine sieve (fine mesh strainer) onto the cold cream and icing sugar and stir well. Pour into six 10 cm (4 in) dariole moulds and allow to cool, then chill in the refrigerator for at least 3 hours.

To serve, dip each mould into hot water for a second or two to loosen the edges. Invert confidently onto a plate. Arrange the blackcurrant compote and shortbread around the panna cotta.

Note: Another variation is to pour the panna cotta mixture into a cooked sweet pastry case, allow to set and then arrange the berries on top. The light, biscuity pastry against the creamy cooked vanilla is glorious.

WILD fennel grows by the sea and in hedgerows, and I often find myself with a small bunch in hand as I walk home from the beach. I love to fill a simple glass vase with it for my kitchen table or to use the pollen, as here, in the most yummy ice cream. It is definitely worth the effort of infusing the fennel pollen with the milk and cream. Delicate and sweet with a delicious honey aniseed flavour.

FENNEL BLOSSOM ICE CREAM

Serves 6

5 egg yolks
100 ml (3½ fl oz/scant ½ cup) runny honey
2 tablespoons brown sugar
250 ml (8½ fl oz/1 cup) whole (full-fat) milk
300 ml (10 fl oz/1¼ cups) double (heavy) cream
4 teaspoons fennel pollen (plus extra to taste)
    or 3–4 heads of fennel
1 teaspoon ground fennel seeds
1 vanilla pod (bean), split and seeds scraped out
fennel blossom, to decorate (or fennel
    seeds if you can't get any)

In a saucepan, whisk the egg yolks together with the honey and sugar, then mix in the milk and cream. Add the fennel pollen, ground fennel seeds and vanilla seeds, and stir constantly over a medium heat until the mixture thickens and becomes like custard.

Strain through a sieve (fine mesh strainer) into a bowl to remove any bits of seed. Allow to cool, then ideally chill in the refrigerator overnight or at least until the mixture is very cold.

When ready, churn in an ice-cream machine according to the manufacturer's instructions, then pour into a small bowl or mould lined with cling film (plastic wrap) and freeze.

Serve on its own in little coupé glasses or on top of treacle tart, decorated with fennel blossom.

Note: To make the ice cream by hand, put a deep baking dish, or a bowl made of plastic or stainless steel in the freezer for 30 minutes allowing it to freeze and then pour your chilled custard mixture into it. After 1 hour remove it from the freezer and stir it with a spatula or whisk, breaking up any frozen icicles. Return it to the freezer, and continue to check the mixture every 30 minutes, stirring as it is freezing, until the ice cream is frozen. It will likely take 2–3 hours to be ready. Place the ice cream in a covered storage container in the freezer, until it is eady to serve.

PEACHES evoke memories for me of sitting outside for breakfast on my grandparents' terrace at their home in the south of France, with the wonderful scent of lavender and rosemary and the sound of the busy crickets.

Peaches are the perfect summer fruit and a peach and almond tart is a lovely end to any meal – a household favourite, especially with my children. Substitute other fruit for the peaches, such as raspberries, apricots, blackberries or plums, depending on the season.

PEACH AND ALMOND TART

Serves 8

6 peaches, washed and sliced
100 g (3½ oz/⅓ cup) apricot jam
pouring cream or a dollop of crème fraîche,
    to serve

For the pastry
250 g (9 oz/2 cups) plain (all-purpose)
    flour, plus extra for dusting
20 g (1 oz/1½ tablespoons) caster (superfine) sugar
1 egg, plus 1 yolk
125 g (4 oz) unsalted butter, diced
1½ teaspoons cold water

For the almond filling
200 g (7 oz) unsalted butter, softened
200 g (7 oz/scant 1 cup) caster (superfine) sugar
2 eggs
200 g (7 oz/2 cups) ground almonds (almond meal)
zest of 1 lemon

First make the pastry. Place the flour in a food processor along with the sugar, whole egg and yolk and diced butter. Blitz. Add the cold water and continue to process until the dough comes together into a smooth ball. Wrap in cling film (plastic wrap) and chill in the refrigerator for 30 minutes while you make the filling.

For the filling, in a large bowl, beat the softened butter together with the sugar until light and fluffy. Beat in the eggs, one at a time, then fold in the ground almonds, until you have a soft paste that quite easily drops from a spoon. Stir in the lemon zest.

continued...

Generously flour your work surface and roll out the pastry large enough to line a 23 cm (9 in) loose-bottomed fluted tart tin (pan). Line the tart tin with the pastry, pressing firmly into the sides with your thumb. Or as pictured, line ten 8 cm (3 in) individual fluted tart cases. Chill for 30 minutes.

Meanwhile, preheat the oven to 190°C (170°C/375°F/Gas 5).

Remove the tart case from the fridge and prick the pastry all over with a fork. Line with baking parchment and fill with baking beans. Bake blind on the middle shelf of the oven for 10–15 minutes, then remove the beans and parchment and return to the oven for another 10 minutes until the pastry is cooked through. If making individual tartlets, reduce the cooking time to 5–10 minutes and 5 minutes.

Remove the tart case from the oven and pour in the almond filling. Arrange the peach slices decoratively on top and return to the middle shelf of the oven. Cook for 35–40 minutes more or until the surface is golden brown and the top is firm to the touch. If making individual tartlets, again reduce the cooking time to 15–20 minutes.

In a small pan, heat the apricot jam until runny, then use a pastry brush to brush it all over the surface of the tart. Leave the tart to cool on a wire rack.

Serve (sliced or as individual tartlets), with a jug of pouring cream or a dollop of crème fraîche on the side.

CERISE Papa, my grandfather, was a wonderful man – a true gentleman who influenced so much of our lives as a family. A twinkle in his eye, a charmer, Papa was more French than the French. He appreciated good food and good wine, and time spent together was always around a table, over long lunches, laughter and fun. Papa used to do this wonderful trick with a cherry – he would place a whole cherry in his mouth, stalk and all, and would be able to take all the flesh off the cherry with the stalk still attached to the pit. It was like magic and as children we just loved watching it. In later years, we realised that it was not as difficult as it looked, but it is a memory that has always stayed with me.

This recipe works just as well with strawberries.

CHERRIES, ELDERFLOWER CORDIAL AND VANILLA ICE CREAM

Serves 4

2 kg (4 lb 8 oz) fresh cherries
4 tablespoons caster (superfine) sugar
200 ml (7 fl oz/scant 1 cup) Harlyn Elderflower Cordial (see page 143)
vanilla ice cream, to serve
fresh elderflowers, to decorate

Wash the cherries and pat them dry, then cut in half and remove the pits. Place in a bowl and sprinkle with the sugar and pour over the elderflower cordial. Allow to sit and infuse for at least 15 minutes, then taste for balance of sweetness.

To serve, simply place in a bowl with a scoop of vanilla ice cream and decorate with fresh elderflowers.

OLD-FASHIONED SPONGE CAKE WITH SUMMER BERRIES AND HOMEMADE JAM

Serves 8–10

4 medium eggs, weighed in their shells
equivalent quantity of unsalted butter
equivalent quantity of soft brown sugar
equivalent quantity of self-raising flour

To decorate
Gooseberry Harvest Jam (see page 208),
    for spreading
1 punnet of fresh seasonal berries, washed
    and sliced (reserve some for decoration)
icing (confectioner's) sugar, for dusting (a great
    way of hiding any imperfections and looks pretty)
sprigs of fresh mint or borage flowers, to decorate

Preheat the oven to 180°C (160°C fan/350°F/Gas 4). Grease and line the bottom and sides of a 7 cm (3 in) deep x 20 cm (8 in) round cake tin (pan) with baking parchment.

First weigh the eggs, and then measure out the rest of your ingredients to the same weight.

In a mixing bowl, beat together the butter and brown sugar until pale and fluffy. Add 1 egg and a heaped tablespoon of flour and mix in well. Add the remaining eggs in the same fashion, then add the rest of the flour and mix until just combined.

Pour into the lined tin and bake for 35–40 minutes or until the sponge springs back to the touch and a skewer inserted to the middle comes out clean. Allow the sponge to cool for 10 minutes, then turn out from the tin onto a wire rack to cool completely.

Once cool, use a serrated knife to slice the sponge in half. Place one disc of the sponge on a cake stand or a favourite plate and spread a thick layer of jam on the top. Use a palette knife to spread the jam out to near the edges. Sprinkle some of the berries on top. Place the other sponge on top and force the jam out of the sides a little. Dust the top and sides with icing sugar, and decorate with berries, sprigs of mint or borage flowers.

Note: Add a layer of whipped cream with the jam for extra indulgence, or a dollop of Cornish clotted cream on the side.

ALWAYS time for cake. This is a wonderful cake that I make time and time again at home. Fill with seasonal berries with lots of homemade jam.

Use the weight of the eggs to determine the weight of the flour, brown sugar and butter.

RITUALS. Making jam, marmalade and compotes is something I find grounding, and what a wonderful way to preserve those delicious fruits of the season. There is nothing better than toast, butter and jam. Preserves also make lovely presents for family or friends, any time of the year – they are joyful. More toast, please.

GOOSEBERRY HARVEST JAM

Makes 1.75 litres (60 fl oz/7½ cups)

1 kg (2 lb 4 oz/8½ cups) gooseberries,
   washed, topped and tailed
150 ml (5 fl oz/scant ⅔ cup) water
1 kg (2 lb 4 oz/4½ cups) caster (superfine) sugar

Place a saucer into the freezer to chill.

Sterilise the jam jars: wash the jars and lids thoroughly in hot, soapy water, then allow them to drip-dry, upside down. Place on a rack in the oven set to 140°C (120°C fan/275°F/Gas ½) for 30 minutes.

Combine the gooseberries and water in a preserving pan or heavy-based saucepan. Bring to the boil, then reduce the heat and simmer for 5–10 minutes until the fruit is softened. Stir in the sugar and cook over a low heat until the sugar has dissolved. Increase the heat and boil rapidly for 8–10 minutes.

To test whether the jam is ready for a set, this is a great method: take the saucer from the freezer and drop a small spoonful of jam onto it. Allow it to cool for a minute, then push your finger through the jam – if it wrinkles, it is good to go; if not, boil for a few more minutes and test for set again.

Once the jam is ready, turn off the heat, skim off any scum from the surface and leave to stand for 15–20 minutes. Spoon the jam into the sterilised jars and seal tightly with the lids while the jam is hot.

Store the Gooseberry Harvest Jam in a cool, dry place and it will keep for up to 6 months. Refrigerate once opened.

FLOWERS Give me flowers every day. The prettiest gin around –
thank you Tinkture. This makes a perfect drink, with a twist of lemon
and rose to dazzle.

ROSE GIN COLLINS
(YES, PLEASE)

Serves 1

lots of ice
100 ml (3½ fl oz/scant ½ cup) Navas
    Cornish Soda Water (or sparkling water)
25 ml (¾ fl oz/1 tablespoon plus 2 teaspoons)
    fresh Harlyn Elderflower Cordial (see page 143)
35 ml (1 fl oz/2 tablespoons plus 1 teaspoon)
    lemon juice
a good glug of Tinkture Cornish Rose Gin
    (or 50 ml/2 fl oz/3½ tablespoons)
1 lemon twirl, to garnish
1 rose petal, for added beauty

First up, put lots of ice into a highball or Collins glass. Then add the
soda or sparkling water, cordial and lemon juice and mix. Gently
pour the rose gin on the top and watch as the golden rose gin
gently meets the lemon mix and starts turning pink.

Taste and consider adding more gin, soda, cordial or ice. Tasting
and considering is a must, obviously. Garnish with the lemon twirl
and rose petal and serve immediately.

AUTUMN
TIDES

AUTUMN TIDES (WILD SWIMMING AT HARLYN BAY)

BEAUTIFUL Cornish autumn is a wonderful season, with its golden light and abundance of produce. A time for gentler flavours. Farmers' markets are aglow with pumpkins, apples and pears, damsons, plums and the last of the tomatoes, gnarly quinces, brambles, field mushrooms, squashes, cabbages and kales.

There is a change in the air – the chaos of summer has disappeared overnight and there seems to be more time. Children return to school and plans to catch up with friends seem possible. Still warm enough to sit outside by day, yet very chilly by night. My childhood memories are of harvest festival at school, of Bonfire Night and trying to write my name in the cold night air with crackling sparklers, of sausages and mash with homemade baked beans, oaty flapjacks, hot chocolate and marshmallows by the fire.

Cornish lanes are quieter and the beaches feel almost deserted compared to the bustling days of summer. I head to the clear blue waters of Harlyn Bay to swim across towards Tide Teller and Big Guns Cove. Walking from Harlyn Beach

House across the fields, over the stiles to the beach, the sand looks and feels like Demerara sugar beneath my feet, soft, sweet and sparkling in the sunshine. The sea is always at its warmest at this time of year, and it feels full of energy. In hues of blue and green, as the waves wash over me, I feel a sense of wellbeing. There is something so healing about being in the sea – nothing makes me feel better than the taste of the water and the salt in my hair.

FOODIE county. Over the years, Cornwall has been known for being home to the culinary best. Long gone are the days when you would only have six months of the year to earn your living. Cornwall has become a destination and home to some of the best-loved British chefs and producers. The Cornish Duck Co. is no exception. The table birds are born to free-range-laying flocks and are reared in a happy environment – so good, and available to buy online. It is so important to know where the food you eat comes from and to support your local farmers. This simple, almost peasant-like, dish is a quick and easy supper that works well throughout the year. I always think of duck as being a special sort of ingredient. It is very easy to cook – it's all in the resting – and is best served pink.

CORNISH DUCK BREAST WITH WHITE BEANS, GARLIC AND ROSEMARY

Serves 2

2 x 250 g (9 oz) free-range duck breasts
2 shallots, thinly sliced
4 garlic cloves, thinly sliced
4 fresh rosemary sprigs, plus extra to garnish
a splash of apple cider vinegar
2 x 560 g (1 lb 4 oz) jars white butter (lima) beans
250 g (9 oz) baby spinach, washed
Cornish sea salt and freshly ground black pepper

Score the skin of the duck breasts at 1.5 cm (½ in) intervals, then season with sea salt and black pepper. Place the duck, skin-side down, in a cold, non-stick frying pan (skillet), then turn the heat to medium–high. Gently cook for 10 minutes without moving the breasts – this is important, as you are rendering out the fat in the skin, which will make the skin golden and crispy.

Turn the duck over and cook for 5 minutes on the other side, then remove to a plate to rest, leaving the pan of duck fat on the heat. Place the shallots and garlic into the hot pan, strip in the rosemary leaves and cook for 4 minutes, gently stirring, until golden brown. Add a splash of vinegar and stir together, then pour in the beans, juice and all. Simmer for a couple of minutes. Just before serving, add the spinach and fold in until just wilted.

Slice the duck breasts at an angle. Divide the beans between bowls and arrange the duck on top, spooning over any resting juices, and garnish with sprigs of rosemary.

DROWNED in cider and cream what else is there. Porthilly shellfish, based at Porthilly on the Camel Estuary, are growers of mussels, oysters, clams and other seasonal produce from the estuary and coastline, including the ever-wonderful samphire (a seaweed-like vegetable, also known as glasswort, foraged at the muddy low tide).

PORTHILLY MUSSELS, LEEKS, CIDER AND CLOTTED CREAM

Serves 6

1 kg (2 lb 4 oz) fresh live mussels (ideally Porthilly)
50 g (2 oz) unsalted butter
1 medium shallot, finely chopped
1 medium leek, washed and finely sliced
2 garlic cloves, finely sliced
300 ml (10 fl oz/1¼ cups) cider
4 tablespoons Cornish clotted cream
3 tablespoons chopped fresh flat-leaf parsley
Cornish sea salt and freshly ground black pepper

Wash the mussels under cold running water and pull off and discard any wispy 'beards' from the shells. Before cooking, you need to make sure all the mussels are alive, so discard any that have broken or cracked shells and any open ones that don't close when tapped on a hard surface

Melt the butter in a very large pan with a lid over a medium heat, add the shallot, leek and garlic and cook for 5 minutes. Pour in the cider, bring to the boil, then add the mussels. Cover and cook for 5–7 minutes, shaking the pan occasionally, until all the mussels have opened. Discard any that are still closed after cooking.

Remove the mussels with a slotted spoon and divide among 6 warmed deep bowls. Return the pan to the heat, bring the cooking liquid to the boil and bubble for 2–3 minutes to reduce. Stir in the cream and parsley, then season the sauce and pour over the mussels.

AUTUMN TIDES

FOYS is where I spent many days as a child. My grandmother had a house on Porthilly Lane and on high days and holidays, if we were not in France, we would be in Cornwall.

The familiar scent of alexanders, campion and cow parsley would perfume the salty air as we approached the beach along the sandy path. I loved the view at low tide across the beach looking towards Padstow, where the estuary would be packed with sailing boats in the height of the season and a sea of buoys in the winter. The rippled sands and casts left behind by lugworms always fascinated me as a child.

I remember taking the ferry to Padstow for crazy golf, ice cream and fudge, and trips to Port Isaac (pictured opposite) for tea with Harold and Joanna, with traditional crab sandwiches and cream tea, all served on Cornish blue china.

Even freezing Cornish days would be spent on the water, learning to sail and water-ski. The wind whipped down the estuary making everything feel so much more challenging. I refused to learn how to capsize in the early days, as the water was too cold.

How happy am I to have found my home here in my adult life. I am now able to see it all with wide eyes, appreciating all its natural beauty, and full of love for the ever-changing weather.

SAFFRON FISH STEW

Serves 4

splash of olive oil
1 garlic clove, sliced
small glass of white wine
1 x 400 g (14 oz) tin good-quality plum tomatoes
bunch of fresh basil, leaves picked and stalks chopped
handful of fennel fronds
2 small monkfish fillets, cut in half
2 small gurnard fillets, cut in half
2 small red mullet fillets (or other firm white fish)
8 tiger prawns (jumbo shrimp), shell on
12 fresh live mussels, cleaned (check they
   are all alive – see page 216)
Cornish sea salt and freshly ground black pepper
4 small slices of crusty bread, to serve
extra virgin olive oil, for drizzling

For the safron aïoli
3 egg yolks
1 garlic clove, peeled
2 pinches of saffron
squeeze of lemon juice
small pinch of Cornish sea salt
200 ml (7 fl oz/scant 1 cup) sunflower oil

First make the saffron aïoli. Put the egg yolks, garlic, saffron, a tiny squeeze of lemon juice and a small pinch of salt in a small food processor. With the motor running, slowly pour in a stream of sunflower oil through the funnel, until the mixture begins to thicken to a mayonnaise consistency. Set aside.

Heat a splash of olive oil in a large, wide saucepan or pot with a lid over a medium heat. Add the sliced garlic and fry until lightly golden. Add the wine, tomatoes, basil and fennel fronds (reserve a few leaves and fronds for garnish) and bring to the boil, then reduce the heat and simmer gently for 10–15 minutes, until the liquid has reduced a little. Add all the fish and shellfish in a single layer and season with salt and pepper. Push the fish down into the liquid and put the lid on the pan. Cook gently for about 10 minutes until the fish and prawns are cooked through.

To serve, toast the bread and warm 4 deep plates. Evenly ladle the fish stew onto the plates. Top each with the reserved basil leaves and fennel fronds, a drizzle of extra virgin olive oil and a big dollop of saffron aïoli on top of the toast. Sometimes, I spoon the aïoli straight into the stew.

Note: If you like, add some halved cooked new potatoes.

BURNISHED with yellow saffron aïoli, my tomato-based fish stew with monkfish, gurnard, red mullet, tiger prawns (jumbo shrimp) and mussels is so pretty and delicious. Fish cookery is something I love and this recipe brings so many of my favourites together. Of course, you can choose to use whatever fish is available and sustainable at different times of the year, so you can really make this dish your own. Buy your fish from sustainable sources (ask your fishmonger), as provenance is so important.

ONE-POT suppers are a perfect way to feed your family at this time of year. I love putting a casserole dish in the middle of the table – it immediately becomes a talking point and heightens the anticipation of sharing and eating together. I always think of Roald Dahl's Willy Wonka and the Chocolate Factory when I cook this dish. This is definitely more luxurious than the cabbage soup that Charlie Bucket's family lived off, as I use cavolo nero, but a little goes a long way. Cabbages are underrated and need to be celebrated, so *HOORAY* for cabbage stew, I promise you will love it.

AUTUMN CAVOLO NERO STEW WITH CHIPOLATAS

Serves 6

2 tablespoons sunflower oil
1 large white onion, thinly sliced
2 garlic cloves, crushed
18 chipolata sausages, cut in half
1 x 400 g (14 oz) tin of chopped tomatoes
500 ml (17 fl oz/2 cups) vegetable stock
1 cavolo nero or Savoy cabbage, shredded
Cornish sea salt and freshly ground black pepper

To serve
250 ml (8½ fl oz/1 cup) crème fraîche
100 g (3½ oz) flat-leaf parsley, roughly chopped

Heat the oil in a large saucepan over a medium heat, then add the onion and garlic and cook until softened. Add the sausages and cook until golden brown. Add the tomatoes and vegetable stock and season to taste with sea salt and black pepper. Finally, add the cavolo nero or cabbage and simmer slowly, uncovered, over a very low heat for 2 hours.

To serve, spoon into bowls and finish with a spoonful of crème fraîche and a sprinkling of parsley. This tastes even better the day after cooking. I have also been known to grate cheese over the top and grill (broil) it – particularly satisfying on a very cold day.

COMFORT *My children have always loved my fish pie recipe. It is always eaten with great happiness and enthusiasm. This fish pie is a no-egg affair – I prefer to have just leeks and fennel running through it, with handfuls of flat-leaf parsley. For a change, spinach and carrot matchsticks work well, too. Fennel is one of my favourite vegetables – it is as good raw as it is gently cooked; so versatile but often forgotten. Crisp and with a subtle aniseed flavour, it works deliciously with the fish. Crème fraîche is always in my storecupboard – richer than soured cream, it enriches this dish perfectly. Undyed smoked haddock always makes the cut for flavour, as does salmon mainly for colour, along with white fish: cod, pollack or ling. This recipe freezes really well, which I have always found useful for those busier days.*

CORNISH FISH PIE WITH SOFT LEEKS AND FENNEL TOPPED WITH SOURDOUGH CRUMBS

Serves 4

200 g (7 oz/2½ cups) fresh sourdough breadcrumbs
2 tablespoons roughly chopped flat-leaf parsley leaves
150 g (5 oz) unsalted butter, melted
2 leeks, thinly sliced
2 garlic cloves, sliced
300 g (10½ oz) fennel with its fronds, finely sliced
650 g (1 lb 7 oz) firm white fish (such as salmon
   or smoked haddock), cut into 2.5 cm (1 in) chunks
1 tablespoon plain (all-purpose) flour
250 g (9 oz/generous 1 cup) crème fraîche
2 tablespoons Dijon mustard
120 ml (4 fl oz/½ cup) water
50 g (2 oz) Parmesan, grated
Cornish sea salt and freshly ground black pepper
hot buttered peas, to serve

Preheat the oven to 200°C (180°C fan/400°F/Gas 6).

Place the breadcrumbs, half of the parsley, half of the butter and a grinding each of salt and pepper in a large bowl and mix to combine. Spread over a large oven tray and bake in the oven for 10 minutes or until golden.

Meanwhile, heat the remaining butter in a large ovenproof or cast-iron pan over a high heat. Add the leeks, garlic and fennel and cook, covered, for 5 minutes or until softened.

Place the fish, flour and some salt and pepper in a large bowl and gently mix to coat. Add the fish mixture, the remaining parsley, crème fraîche, mustard and water to the pan and stir to combine. Top with the golden breadcrumbs and Parmesan and transfer to the oven to cook for a further 10 minutes or until golden brown and cooked through.

Sprinkle with more black pepper and serve with hot buttered peas. Evie always reaches for the ketchup, every time.

Note: If freezing, do so without the topping (which is best made when needed as the sourdough crumbs will become soggy when defrosted). Allow the pie to cool for 2 hours, then wrap with a double layer of cling film (plastic wrap) and a layer of foil before placing in the freezer. This pie can be frozen for up to 3 months.

AUTUMN TIDES

THE SOFT and gentle flavours of autumn days – pumpkins, squashes and beetroot (beets) all bring a sense of excitement to my kitchen. This soup recipe is quick and simple and really champions autumn. I have also added the mighty celeriac – agreed, it's not much of a looker, but I think it's so versatile with a wonderful texture that sits in good company with the pumpkin. The deep orange colour of this soup will bring warmth and happiness to any table.

AN AUTUMN SOUP WITH PUMPKIN, CELERIAC AND CRISPY SAGE

Serves 4

6 tablespoons olive oil
1 medium onion, chopped
1 litre (34 fl oz/4 cups) chicken or vegetable stock
500 g (1 lb 2 oz) pumpkin, peeled and deseeded,
    cut into even-sized small cubes
300 g celeriac (celery root), peeled and cut into
    even-sized small cubes
8 sage leaves
Cornish sea salt and freshly ground black pepper

Heat 2 tablespoons of the olive oil in a large saucepan over a medium heat, add the onion and cook for 5–10 minutes until soft and translucent but not brown (never rush an onion). Add the stock and bring to a simmer, then add the pumpkin and celeriac cubes and cook for 15–20 minutes until soft but still holding their shape. Add a good pinch of salt and a couple of twists of pepper.

Transfer the mixture to a blender or food processor and blitz until smooth.

Heat the remaining 4 tablespoons of olive oil in a shallow frying pan (skillet) over a medium heat and gently fry the sage leaves until crisp.

Pour the pumpkin soup back into the pan and warm through, then taste for seasoning. Serve in your favourite bowls, topped with the crispy sage.

Drop of Civrac

WINE and food have always been an important part of my life. So meeting Mark and falling in love with this incredible person was life changing. Mark is a Cornishman, a winemaker, scientist, artist and occasional chef who is passionate about wine, art and surfing. We combine our time between Cornwall and the rolling hills and vineyards of Bordeaux: two places we love.

Days spent among the vines of Château Civrac were wonderful. Watching and learning the process of winemaking was so exciting, yet so involved, scientific and practical – a labour of love. They say that anything that looks effortless is usually hard work.

Life on the vineyard was romantic and idyllic, but really it was just like farming, with so many challenges and a market that is so competitive. Mark sold the vineyard in 2018 and one day may return to winemaking, but for now we can enjoy his wines and other adventures together.

In the late autumn of 2016, I was lucky enough to make my own vintage. I embraced all the tasks of fermentation, *remontage* and *pigéage* with enthusiasm and vigour. I loved the process of winemaking and am very proud of $(E + M)^2$ – the name chosen by Mark, bearing our initials and the fraction giving a nod to Mark's scientific background. The result was a light Malbec blended 60/40 with Merlot, raspberry and cherry on the nose, leading to tobacco and spice. It is light in the mouth with juicy acidity and a subtle vanilla finish.

Matching food and wine is a highlight for us. As a winemaker, Mark has worked with some great chefs and restaurants and that is how we ended up meeting like-minded people with a love for bringing people around a table to enjoy wine, food and conversation. It is one of life's simple pleasures that brings us great joy.

Mark encouraged me to write this book – quietly telling me to just get on with it whenever I wobbled or lost my creativity. He also makes the most delicious wine, believing that the label should reflect the style of wine inside the bottle and that the wine should reflect where it is made, how it is made and some of the character of the winemaker themself. What an amazing achievement – I am so proud to be part of his life.

One day, soon, we may find ourselves among the vines once more.

POMMES, pommes and more pommes, I would not be able to tell you how many apples Sophie and I peeled at the old antique table at L'Etape... many! A classic tarte tatin was always on the menu for the guests, and was a particular hit with the ouvriers (workers) who would come in for their lunch on weekdays. Jean-Philippe, Jean-Jaques, Richard, Thierry, Monsieur Soufflé, Mimil the 'thirsty' Frenchman on his moped, Baby Rose (the butcher) – all larger-than-life characters that I find mirrored here in Cornwall in the same rural kind of life.

I wait with anticipation as the autumn days arrive and my thoughts turn to apples, pears, quinces and plums. I find Braeburn or russet apples work well in my tarte tatin. Pack the apples together tightly. Dark caramel, sweet sweet apple and crisp pastry – delicious.

TARTE TATIN WITH POMMES

Serves 4–6

flour, for dusting
500 g (1 lb 2 oz) ready-made puff pastry
100 g (3½ oz/scant ½ cup) caster (superfine) sugar
100 ml (3½ fl oz/scant ½ cup) Calvados
1 vanilla pod (bean), split lengthways and seeds scraped
50 g (2 oz) unsalted butter
6 eating apples, peeled, halved horizontally and cored

Preheat the oven to 200°C (180°C fan/400°F/Gas 6).

Dust a work surface with flour and roll the pastry out with a rolling pin to 1 cm (½ in) thick and large enough to cover an ovenproof or cast-iron frying pan (skillet), with 5 cm (2 in) of extra pastry around the edge. Set aside.

Set the frying pan over a medium heat and add the sugar, Calvados, vanilla seeds and pod. Let the sugar dissolve and cook until the liquid forms a light caramel. Once the caramel has turned a chesnut-brown colour, carefully add the butter and arrange the halved apples in the pan, packing them in tightly, cut-sides down. Take care, as the caramel will be extremely hot. Lay the pastry over the top and tuck it in around the edges. A wooden spoon works well for this, so you don't have to touch the caramel.

Bake the tarte in the oven for 25–30 minutes until the pastry is golden brown and sticky with caramel. Remove from the oven and allow to cool slightly before turning it out. Have a plate larger than your pan, put it on top of the pan and confidently turn it over. Again, be careful, as the caramel will be hot. Allow to cool.

Note: Serve with vanilla ice cream, with a Calvados or a Pineau served over ice to drink.

SOUND of the wood pigeon outside my window, the smell of straw through the streets. When I was 16, I went to help out at L'Etape, a bijou hotel restaurant in Blanot, a village near Mâcon deep in the heart of the Burgundy countryside. It was a place I grew to love and that gave me a platform of experience and skills for my future. We cooked up a storm and I loved the way of life there, from the early markets to the late-night gangets (discos). Jean-Christophe and Sophie gave me an opportunity to find my way in life – we laughed, we cried, we worked hard and created a wonderful place with many happy memories.

AUTUMN TIDES

I LOVE a tiramisu: chocolate, cream, mascarpone, boudoir biscuits (sponge fingers), coffee and booze – it's a classic. I keep it to two tiers, with a strong dusting of cocoa powder on top to finish. Perfect as a make-ahead pudding, make in a single large dish or individual Kilner jars or pots.

I use to give my children boudoir biscuits when they were babies, especially when they were teething. These days, that would be frowned on, as they are so sugary.

TIRAMISU

Serves 6

250 ml (8½ fl oz/1 cup) freshly made espresso
   (I like to use Yallah espresso)
250 ml (8½ fl oz/1 cup) double (heavy) cream
250 g (9 oz/generous 1 cup) mascarpone
200 g (7 oz/scant 1 cup) caster (superfine) sugar
75 ml (2½ fl oz/5 tablespoons) Marsala wine
2 teaspoons vanilla extract
40 boudoir biscuits/sponge fingers
50 g (2 oz) dark chocolate (54 per cent cocoa solids)
2 tablespoons cocoa powder

Pour the espresso into a shallow dish and allow to cool.

Meanwhile, beat together the double cream, mascarpone, sugar, Marsala and vanilla in a large bowl until smooth. I like my tiramisu quite boozy, so add the Marsala gradually, taste and consider the flavour, and you can always add a little more if you like. Set aside.

Dip the sponge fingers into the cooled espresso until just soaked through, not soggy. Layer half of the soaked sponge fingers into a large serving dish (or individual jars, if using) and then spread over half of the mascarpone and cream. Repeat to form a second layer, then grate the chocolate on top. To finish, dust over the cocoa powder.

Cover and ideally refrigerate for a few hours, or overnight, before serving.

RICH, yet subtle and light, this mousse has been on my menu since the beginning. At The Harbour, my restaurant in Port Isaac situated on the platt looking out to sea, is where my cooking style began to take shape. It was a bijou place with 26 covers, housed in a unique, quirky building among the slate-topped houses of Port Isaac. One of my customers requested vanilla ice cream on top of his mousse instead of clotted cream, and from that day forward it always appeared on my menu like that. The taste of chocolate against the cold, sweet, vanilla-y ice cream is a triumph.

RICH CHOCOLATE MOUSSE WITH VANILLA ICE CREAM AND BAKED QUINCE

Serves 4–6

200 g (7 oz) good-quality dark chocolate
    (at least 54 per cent cocoa solids)
2 tablespoons water
4 eggs, separated
200 ml (7 fl oz/scant 1 cup) double (heavy) cream
pinch of Cornish sea salt
2 tablespoons caster (superfine) sugar

To serve
vanilla ice cream or Cornish clotted cream
Baked Quince (see page 234)

Melt the chocolate together with the water in a heatproof bowl set over a pan of barely simmering water (make sure the base of the bowl doesn't touch the water). When the mixture is smooth and shiny, lift the bowl off the pan and beat in the egg yolks.

In a separate bowl, whip the cream to soft peaks, then gently fold it into the chocolate mixture.

In a third very clean mixing bowl, whisk the egg whites with the salt to soft peaks, then gradually whisk in the sugar. Carefully fold the egg whites in 2 additions into the chocolate mixture. The first addition will loosen the chocolate, the second will make it light.

Pour into individual French glasses or small Kilner (Mason) jars and chill in the refrigerator for 1 hour.

Serve, topped with vanilla ice cream or a dollop my favourite Cornish clotted cream, with the baked quince on the side.

IN LATE September to early October, the first quince fruits begin to ripen – a welcome to the ever-beautiful, ever-changing season that slowly unfolds in a burst of colour across the land. Slowly baked, their delicious fudge-like texture eats wonderfully well with my Chocolate Mousse (see page 233). Poached apples and pears work well, too.

THE UNDERRATED BAKED QUINCE

Serves 4

4 quinces
225 g (8 oz/1 cup) caster (superfine) sugar
zest of 1 lemon
2 fresh bay leaves
1 vanilla pod (bean), split
120 ml (4 fl oz/½ cup) water

Preheat the oven to 150°C (130°C fan/300°F/Gas 1).

Rinse and wipe the quinces clean. Quarter them lengthways but do not remove the pith or core. Put the quarters, cut-sides up, in a baking tray (pan), sprinkle over the sugar and lemon zest and add the bay leaves and vanilla. Pour in the water, cover lightly with kitchen foil and bake in the oven for 2 hours, turning the fruit a couple of times.

When the quinces are soft, sticky and a beautiful burnt orange colour, they are ready.

ON COLDER DAYS, poached fruit works so well with this recipe, and one of my favourites is slowly baked quinces. I'm so fortunate that my good friends, Stanley, David and Michael from Woolpit, always arrive in the autumn bringing me apples, pears and quinces from their beautiful garden.

QUINCES are the gnarly, slightly misunderstood fruit that appear in the autumn months. They have a natural bouquet – place two or three in a bowl and you will find your house filled with a scent of beautiful floral tones, vanilla, pear and coconut. Slowly baking them is life enhancing and something you will always look forward to when autumn arrives, I promise.

A LESSON IN SIMPLICITY.

Well, I was quite overly excited the day I was asked to appear on one of the most popular food programmes on TV, *The Great British Menu* – not just a programme, but a competition, up against top chefs from the South West and beyond. I thrive off pressure and love challenging myself, so I instantly agreed to do it, exclaiming, 'enthusiam moves the world', in the VT for my test run. The brief was 'music', so my desert-island dishes were up for scrutiny. I made a pudding course called Disco Fever, featuring a blackberry ice cream. I tested all my recipes for days in the run-up to the competition. On the first attempt at making this ice cream, it came out the most unattractive tone of purple. Oscar, Finn and Evie looked at me – their faces said it all. Finn, always the most honest, said, 'Mother you can do better than this'. So, I tweaked the ingredients, added a little more crème de cassis (of course), and it came out the most beautiful creamy pink lilac colour, lifting my dish to new heights.

I think I came out unscathed from the whole experience. I was disappointed that I had not made it further through the competition, but I was pleased that I had stuck to my way of cooking and my ethos of beautiful pared-back food.

DISCO FEVER. This recipe transports me back to my childhood. It's an ice cream that will fill you with happiness. You'll need to prepare the ice cream a day in advance as the mixture needs to chill overnight before churning.

To make vanilla ice cream just omit the blackberry purée, and to make the ice cream by hand, see the note on page 198.

BLACKBERRY ICE CREAM

Serves 6

400 ml (13 fl oz/generous 1½ cups) double
  (heavy) cream
350 ml (12 fl oz/scant 1½ cups) milk
1 vanilla pod (bean), split
6 egg yolks
125 g (4 oz/generous ½ cup) caster (superfine) sugar
2 tablespoons crème de cassis

For the purée
1 kg (2 lb 4 oz) frozen blackberries
4 tablespoons caster (superfine) sugar

Start with the purée. Put the blackberries into a heavy-based saucepan along with the sugar and gently warm through, allowing the sugar to dissolve and the fruit to bleed. Use a stick blender or a food processor to blend the mixture into a smooth purée and then pass through a sieve (fine mesh strainer) into a bowl to remove any pips (seeds). Cover and set aside in the fridge.

For the ice cream, pour the cream and milk into a heavy-based pan, add the vanilla pod and slowly bring to simmering point. Remove from the heat and set aside to infuse for 10 minutes, then strain the mixture into a clean pan.

In a large bowl, whisk together the egg yolks and sugar, then pour in the warm cream mixture, stirring continuously. Pour back into the saucepan and heat gently until the mixture thickens enough so that when you run your finger through it on the back of a wooden spoon it leaves a clear trail. Allow to cool, then refrigerate overnight.

The next day, gradually fold the blackberry purée and crème de cassis into the cream mixture and taste to check the balance of sweetness. Churn the mixture in an ice cream machine until thick and creamy, according to the manufacturer's instructions.

When ready to eat, scoop into bowls and enjoy.

HIGH days and holidays, and early morning walks to the bakery with my Dadio (my dad) for the best teatime treats. Nothing evokes more Cornish childhood memories for me than the quintessential cream tea.

I love baking, and splits, donuts and scones are so worth making yourself. Here are my warm splits, with jam and clotted cream. I think a revival of the split is required. I love them and, of course, it almost goes without saying... Jam first. These are delicious with strawberry, raspberry or damson jam.

CORNISH SPLITS, RASPBERRY JAM, CORNISH CLOTTED CREAM

Makes 12

28 g (1 oz) fresh yeast
2 teaspoons caster (superfine) sugar
275 ml (9½ fl oz/scant 1¼ cups) milk, warmed
450 g (1 lb/3¼ cups) strong (bread) strong flour,
    plus extra for dusting
115 g (4 oz/1 cup) plain (all-purpose) flour
85 g (3 oz) salted butter

To serve
raspberry jam
Cornish clotted cream

Preheat the oven to 180°C (160°C fan/350°F/Gas 4).

First, mix the yeast and sugar together with the warm milk until blended (if the milk is too hot it will kill the yeast, so just warm it to hand-hot).

In a large bowl, sift together the flours, then rub in the butter until it resembles breadcrumbs. Make a well in the middle, pour in the milky mixture and work into a dough with your hands. Knead for about 10 minutes, then set aside, covered with a damp dish towel, and allow to rise in a warm place for about 1 hour until doubled in size.

Knock back and knead again for about 10 minutes (I see this as a mini workout), then form your dough into 12 buns using a plain round scone cutter. Place on a floured baking sheet, cover with a damp dish towel and leave to prove for an hour until doubled in size.

Bake in the oven for 20 minutes. Remove from the oven and cover with a damp dish towel for about 15 minutes so that they do not develop a crust.

You can keep these little buns for up to 4 days in an airtight container.

Serve warm, with homemade good-quality raspberry jam and Cornish clotted cream. Add the jam first.

If you do not get cream on your nose when you eat them, you do not have enough cream on the split.

MY GO-TO PUDDING, delicious served with my Crème Anglaise (see page 35) and often on my menu at the St. Tudy Inn. I highly recommend buying whole almonds and blitzing them up yourself – you get a coarser texture in the cake, which is lovely. This gluten-free pudding is fudgy but so light, and delicious warm from the oven. One piece is never enough.

FLOURLESS CHOCOLATE AND ALMOND PUDDING

Serves 8–10

160 g (5½ oz) good-quality dark chocolate,
   broken up
pinch of Cornish sea salt
160 g (5½ oz) cold unsalted butter, cut into
   pieces, plus extra for buttering
4 eggs, separated
125 g (4 oz/generous ½ cup) caster (superfine) sugar
160 g (5½ oz/1½ cups) ground almonds (almond meal)
   (or whole almonds, blitzed up)

Preheat the oven to 180°C (160°C fan/350°F/Gas 4). Butter a 23 cm (9 in) round cake tin (pan) and line the base with baking parchment.

Combine the chocolate and salt in a heatproof bowl and set over a pan of simmering water. When the chocolate has melted, turn off the heat and drop the butter pieces into the bowl. Do not stir. Let the mixture sit for a few minutes until the butter begins to melt, then stir through and leave for another few minutes. Stirring too much will cool the chocolate too quickly.

In a separate bowl, whisk the egg whites to soft peaks. Add the sugar and whisk until stiff peaks form.

Now stir the chocolate mixture until the butter is melted. Use a whisk to stir in the egg yolks, one at a time, then gently fold in the egg whites. Fold in the ground almonds, being careful not to overmix and knock the air out of the mixture.

Pour the mixture into the prepared tin and bake for 25 minutes, or until an inserted skewer comes out clean. Remove from the oven and allow to cool before turning out.

Note: Delicious served with Crème Anglaise (see page 35).

SUPPLIERS

FAVOURITES

Coombeshead Bakery
Inhabiting the same converted barn space as the restaurant at Coombeshead Farm, the bakery is headed up by Ben Glazer. Ben uses heritage varieties of wheat, spelt and rye, all farmed organically, for his sourdough wares.
www.coombesheadfarm.co.uk

Cornish Sea Salt
Turning tides to sea salt differently
www.cornishseasalt.co.uk

Just Shellfish Port Isaac
Fresh crab and lobster in the heart of Port Isaac.
justshellfish.co.uk

Mark Hellyar Wine
Find Mark's wines here
www.markhellyarwine.co.uk

Matthew Stevens
Fresh fish and seafood specialists.
www.matthewstevens-cornishfish.com

Padstow Kitchen Garden
Located at Trerethern Farm in Padstow overlooking the Camel Estuary, Ross Geach grows a huge variety of vegetables over several acres here. Ross is passionate about growing and supplies to some of the finest restaurants across the land.
www.padstowkitchengarden.co.uk

Porthilly Shellfish
Based in Porthilly on the Camel Estuary.
www.porthillyshellfish.com

St. Enodoc Asparagus
The finest around, grown close to the sea, where the salty air enhances the flavour. Jax Buse has been growing these beautiful spears at Great Keiro Farm for over 20 years. They will send freshly cut asparagus straight to your door. I always treat asparagus like fresh flowers and place it upright in a jug of water – this helps it keep longer, although it never lasts that long in our house.
www.st-enodoc-asparagus.uk

Tinkture
Organic rose gin, hand-crafted in Cornwall, made with fresh David Austin roses, which turn it pink. My drinks cupboard would be empty without this beauty.
www.wearetinkture.com

Yallah Coffee Roasters
Single origin coffee roasted in Cornwall. Partnered with Trees for Life, the reforesting conservation charity.
www.yallahcoffee.co.uk

MORE FAVOURITE THINGS, PEOPLE AND PLACES

Atelier Ellis
Paint studio with a carefully selected palette
of handmade paint to tell the story of homo.
www.atelierellis.co.uk

Busby & Fox
Independent fashion and lifestyle brand
by Emma Vowles.
www.busbyandfox.com

Cut By Beam
Always making. Specialists in laser-cutting.
www.cutbybeam.co.uk

Edith and Bertha
Garments made in Penryn, West Cornwall.
@edithandbertha_dressmaker

The Garden Baker
Beautifully designed cakes.
@thegardenbaker

Garden Gate Flower Co.
Floral studio, garden and school by
Rebecca Stuart.
www.thegardengateflowercompany.co.uk

George's Surf School
Private surf coaching.
www.georgessurfschool.com

Rowen and Wren
Here is to a life more beautifully lived.
www.rowenandwren.co.uk.

Justine Tabak
A slow fashion collection, carefully made
in the British Isles.
www.justinetabak.co.uk

Katie Childs Cliffside Gallery
A unique working studio in Port Isaac.
www.cliffsidegallery.com

Kurt Jackson
A leading British contemporary artist.
www.jacksonfoundationgallery.com

Land and Water
Born on the shoreline, beautiful bath
and body products.
www.land-and-water.co.uk

Molesworth and Bird
Obsessed with seaweed, they collect,
press it and create beautiful things.
www.molesworthandbird.com

Nicole Heidaripour
Beautiful drawings that bring style and
much happiness.
www.Nicoleheidaripour.com

Prindl Pottery
Cornish potter, trained in Japan and the US,
known for fine dishes and glazes.
www.prindlpottery.co.uk

Robert Welch Designs
The perfect cutlery.
www.robertwelch.com

Savernake Knives
www.savernakeknives.co.uk

Sophie Conran China
Beautiful things
www.sophieconran.com

Watergate Bay Hotel
Contemporary hotel on the Cornwall coast.
All about the balance of life.
www.watergatebay.co.uk

WoodEdit
Simple, stylish and handmade English
furniture that I would not be without.
www.woodedit.co.uk

EMILY SCOTT

Lockdown. My rooms and restaurant at the St. Tudy Inn remain closed. This is a very hard and uncertain time, as reopening with social distancing in place is just not operationally viable, even when I am given the green light to reopen. Time will tell what happens. I feel bereft. Everything I had set my sights on and that I felt defined me has abruptly stopped. The lights have not just been dimmed, they have been switched off. It is a waiting game and all I can do is have everything in place to bounce back. As I write, we are all still living in lockdown. Some measures have been eased, but I think we all have to accept that recovery from this global pandemic is going to be slow and with a new normal; we have to adapt and diversify.

I vividly remember the email pinging into my inbox in January 2020. Little did I know, or the rest of the world for that matter, that 2020 was going to be life changing and bring so many challenges to everyone. I had been offered the wonderful opportunity of opening a pop-up restaurant on the beach at Watergate Bay, the place that the iconic restaurant, Fifteen, called home for many years. I did not hesitate to say yes. I replied straightaway, surprising myself with my boldness and lack of hesitation. This project was an opportunity to find my way back to the sea and shore. I did the numbers and agreed a deal... and then lockdown arrived, which changed everything.

Zoom meetings began and a whole new way of communicating. The constant speculation, the financial worry and then the relief, too, of being able to stop, slow down and appreciate things more. Time to write, time to start new projects, time to reassess, time with my children, real quality time that will be precious forever. In moments, a summer holiday that seemed to last forever.

Deliberation followed, but I decided to go for it, not knowing when I would be allowed to open and what hospitality would look like with strict social distancing measures in place. The earliest date we had all been given for potential reopening was July 4.

Restaurants, to me, had always been a place to gather, share good food and wine at a table together. The new words on the block were 'social distancing' and the '2-metre rule', which was something that was in constant discussion, the safety of my guests and team being paramount.

I held the keys for this amazing venue in my hands – a new chapter and new hope. It was all about keeping my team small, and much love and support from our customers, old and new, was needed to make it work. Lockdown spirit, rush slowly, waste less and care for each other. A new appreciation of our world and what it has to offer. The connection between the land and water. An ethos close to my heart was the way forward. Stripping things back, keeping it simple and seeking quality local suppliers, knowing the story, the provenance of how food found its way to the table.

Returning to the seaside for a one-off, limited-edition opportunity. The future suddenly appeared full of colour, new energy and excitement. In July, August and September I was heading back to the ocean and Emily Scott Food Cornwall was a go.

SEASIDE DAYS

I am excited to be returning to Watergate Bay and opening a restaurant on the sea wall. I will have the same 'less-is-more' ethos, using locally sourced ingredients, a stripped-back and simple seafood- and plant-based menu, seaweed on the walls and flowers on the tables. Come and find us at the beach.

www.emilyscottfood.com

ABOUT EMILY

To put it simply, Emily is passionate about food and it is in her kitchen where she feels most at home. She loves nothing more than delighting others through food, bringing friends and family together around the table.

Emily's passion for the connection between food, a sense of place and storytelling is infectious, intriguing and comforting all at the same time. Her story is one which interweaves the sentimental tales of a childhood in Provence with her grandfather 'Papa' collecting strawberries from the fields to the hum of crickets in the warm sunshine, to the beautiful shores of Cornwall and golden sandy beaches. Experience and memories are translated into ingredients which collectively are heightening into simplistic, rustic dishes which are easily recreated at home.

EMILY SCOTT

INDEX

almonds: almond and pistachio
    biscotti 142
    flourless chocolate and
        almond pudding 242
    granola with almonds and
        pecans 60
    peach and almond tart 202–4
    pistachio nut pudding 63
amaretti crumble crisp 39
anchovies: green sauce for
        everything, or salsa verde
        44
apples: pain perdu (lost bread)
        pudding 79
    tarte tatin with pommes
        230–1
artichokes: hot artichoke dip 89
    salad of baby artichokes,
        asparagus, leaves and quail
        eggs with lemon dressing
        and carta di musica
        117–18
asparagus: roasted asparagus
        128
    salad of baby artichokes,
        asparagus, leaves and quail
        eggs with lemon dressing
        and carta di musica 117–18

bacon: boeuf bourguignon,
        chestnut mushrooms,
        lardons with winter herbs
        68
barbecues 154
beans: Cornish duck breast with
        white beans, garlic and
        rosemary 214
biscuits: almond and pistachio
        biscotti 142
    brown sugar shortbread stars
        39
    Cornish fairings 134
    dark chocolate and oat
        cookies 41
blackcurrants: vanilla-seeded
        panna cotta and
        blackcurrant compote
        with brown sugar
        shortbread 196–7
bread: eggy bread 108
    English cucumber
        sandwiches with salted
        butter 49

pain perdu (lost bread)
        pudding 79
    salad of baby artichokes,
        asparagus, leaves and quail
        eggs with lemon dressing
        and carta di musica 117–18
    smoked salmon pinwheels 88

cakes: chocolate and hazelnut
        brownies 133
    Cornish splits, raspberry jam,
        Cornish clotted cream
        240–1
    flourless chocolate and
        almond pudding 242
    golden syrup flapjacks, good
        for any day 38
    old-fashioned sponge cake
        with summer berries and
        homemade jam 206–7
    pistachio nut pudding 63
    spiced carrot cake with
        cream cheese and butter
        icing 8–10
carrots: glazed carrots 43
    spiced carrot cake with
        cream cheese and butter
        icing 8–10
    summer carrot salad with
        flat-leaf parsley and
        wholegrain dressing 191
carta di musica: salad of baby
        artichokes, asparagus,
        leaves and quail eggs with
        lemon dressing and carta
        di musica 117–18
cavolo nero: autumn cavolo
        nero stew with chipolatas
        223
celeriac: an autumn soup with
        pumpkin, celeriac and
        crispy sage 226
Cheddar: Keen's Cheddar on
        toast with sweet leeks 50
    little gem tart with Keen's
        Cheddar, spring onions
        and flat-leaf parsley 123
cherries, elderflower cordial and
        vanilla ice cream 205
chicken: chicken with orange,
        cream and tarragon 74–5
    Marnie's chicken soup with
        wild garlic, spinach and
        spring herbs 125–6

spring roast chicken with wild
        garlic, herbs, roast new
        potatoes and tarragon
        mayo 120
chipolatas: autumn cavolo nero
        stew with chipolatas 223
chives 34
    buttered peas with parsley
        and chives 42
chocolate: chocolate and
        hazelnut brownies 133
    chocolate and hazelnut fudge
        36
    dark chocolate and oat
        cookies 41
    English strawberries dipped in
        dark chocolate 175
    flourless chocolate and
        almond pudding 242
    rich chocolate mousse with
        vanilla ice cream and baked
        quince 233
chorizo: monkfish, Cornish
        chorizo and sun blush
        tomatoes on rosemary
        skewers 158
cloves: Christmas glazed ham
        with clementines and
        cloves 92–3
    orange clove pomanders 98
coconut: Cornish fairings 134
coffee: simply affogato 136
    tiramisu 232
condensed milk: chocolate and
        hazelnut fudge 36
coriander 34
Cornish pasties 76–7
courgettes: Port Isaac
        mackerel with a raw
        salad of courgettes, chilli,
        nasturtium flowers and
        rocket 150
crab: Cornish crab linguine with
        chilli, lemon and parsley
        104
    Port Isaac crab, toast and
        mayo 54
cream: blackberry ice cream 239
    chicken with orange, cream
        and tarragon 74–5
    citrusy lemon posset 132
    crème Anglaise or English
        cream 35
    crème chantilly 38

meringue roulade with clementine curd, cream and passion fruit 96–8
pain perdu (lost bread) pudding 79
pavlova with whipped cream, poached rhubarb and pistachios 138
thick vanilla custard 35
cream cheese: spiced carrot cake with cream cheese and butter icing 8–10
crème Anglaise or English cream 35
crème chantilly 38
crème fraîche: cool cucumber salad with crème fraîche and dill 161
jammy fig tart topped with crème fraîche and lavender flowers 178
cucumber: cool cucumber salad with crème fraîche and dill 161
English cucumber sandwiches with salted butter 49
custard: crème Anglaise or English cream 35
thick vanilla custard 35

decorations: dried orange garlands 90–1
orange clove pomanders 98
desserts: blackberry ice cream 239
amaretti crumble crisp 39
candy pink rhubarb compote 136
cherries, elderflower cordial and vanilla ice cream 205
citrusy lemon posset 132
crème Anglaise or English cream 35
English strawberries dipped in dark chocolate 175
fennel blossom ice cream 198
flourless chocolate and almond pudding 242
jammy fig tart topped with crème fraîche and lavender flowers 178
lemon mascarpone tart 80
meringue roulade with clementine curd, cream and passion fruit 96–8

pain perdu (lost bread) pudding 79
pavlova with whipped cream, poached rhubarb and pistachios 138
peach and almond tart 202–4
pistachio nut pudding 63
rich chocolate mousse with vanilla ice cream and baked quince 233
simply affogato 136
summer fruit jelly with whole English strawberries and vanilla ice cream 176
tarte tatin with pommes 230–1
thick vanilla custard 35
tiramisu 232
vanilla-seeded panna cotta and blackcurrant compote with brown sugar shortbread 196–7
dips: hot artichoke dip 89
drinks: Harlyn elderflower cordial 143
rose gin Collins 209
duck: Cornish duck breast with white beans, garlic and rosemary 214

eggs: crème Anglaise or English cream 35
eggy bread 108
lemon mascarpone tart 80
meringue roulade with clementine curd, cream and passion fruit 96–8
pain perdu (lost bread) pudding 79
pavlova with whipped cream, poached rhubarb and pistachios 138
pistachio nut pudding 63
scrambled eggs, wilted wild garlic, sourdough toast 109
tarragon mayo 43
thick vanilla custard 35
elderflowers: Harlyn elderflower cordial 143

fennel: Cornish fish pie with soft leeks and fennel topped with sourdough crumbs 224–5
fennel and Parmesan gratin 73

fennel blossom ice cream 198
feta: red Camargue rice with feta and summer herb salad 166
figs 34
fig jam 129
jammy fig tart topped with crème fraîche and lavender flowers 178
fish: Cornish fish pie with soft leeks and fennel topped with sourdough crumbs 224–5
lemon sole, herb dressing, watercress and sea herbs 64
Mr Dory, John Dory simply roasted with lemon and thyme 194
Port Isaac mackerel with a raw salad of courgettes, chilli, nasturtium flowers and rocket 150
saffron fish stew 220–1
smoked salmon pinwheels 88
flapjacks: golden syrup flapjacks, good for any day 38
flowers 33–4
courgette-flower risotto 188
Harlyn elderflower cordial 143
jammy fig tart topped with crème fraîche and lavender flowers 178
Port Isaac mackerel with a raw salad of courgettes, chilli, nasturtium flowers and rocket 150
fudge: chocolate and hazelnut fudge 36

garlic: Cornish duck breast with white beans, garlic and rosemary 214
hand-dived Cornish scallops, pan-fried with thyme, garlic and butter 114
Marnie's chicken soup with wild garlic, spinach and spring herbs 125–6
roast new potatoes with thyme and garlic 42
scrambled eggs, wilted wild garlic, sourdough toast 109
slow-roasted lamb shoulder with smoked paprika, garlic and thyme 110

spring roast chicken with wild garlic, herbs, roast new potatoes and tarragon mayo 120

weekend spaghetti with garlic and chilli 113

gin: rose gin Collins 209

goat's cheese: Vulscombe goat's cheese and caramelised red onion tartlets 86

golden syrup flapjacks, good for any day 38

gooseberry harvest jam 208

granola with almonds and pecans 60

ham: Christmas glazed ham with clementines and cloves 92–3

hazelnuts: chocolate and hazelnut brownies 133

chocolate and hazelnut fudge 36

herbs 33–4

ice cream: blackberry ice cream 239

cherries, elderflower cordial and vanilla ice cream 205

fennel blossom ice cream 198

simply affogato 136

summer fruit jelly with whole English strawberries and vanilla ice cream 176

ingredients 31, 32–4

jam: fig jam 129

gooseberry harvest jam 208

jelly: summer fruit jelly with whole English strawberries and vanilla ice cream 176

John Dory: Mr Dory, John Dory simply roasted with lemon and thyme 194

lamb: slow-roasted lamb shoulder with smoked paprika, garlic and thyme 110

leeks: Cornish fish pie with soft leeks and fennel topped with sourdough crumbs 224–5

Keen's Cheddar on toast with sweet leeks 50

Porthilly mussels, leeks, cider and clotted cream 216

lemons: citrusy lemon posset 132

lemon mascarpone tart 80

lettuce: little gem tart with Keen's Cheddar, spring onions and flat-leaf parsley 123

lobster: Port Isaac lobster over fire with fines herbes 157

mackerel: Port Isaac mackerel with a raw salad of courgettes, chilli, nasturtium flowers and rocket 150

marshmallows: toasted giant marshmallows 160

mascarpone: lemon mascarpone tart 80

tiramisu 232

mayonnaise: tarragon mayo 43

meringues: meringue roulade with clementine curd, cream and passion fruit 96–8

pavlova with whipped cream, poached rhubarb and pistachios 138

milk: blackberry ice cream 239

flat-leaf parsley sauce 95

pain perdu (lost bread) pudding 79

porridge, gold top milk, Demerara and roasted plums with bay and vanilla 62

thick vanilla custard 35

monkfish, Cornish chorizo and sun blush tomatoes on rosemary skewers 158

mozzarella: buffalo mozzarella, broad bean, olive, lemon and rocket salad 185

mushrooms: boeuf bourguignon, chestnut mushrooms, lardons with winter herbs 68

mussels: Porthilly mussels, leeks, cider and clotted cream 216

saffron fish stew 220–1

oats: dark chocolate and oat cookies 41

golden syrup flapjacks, good for any day 38

granola with almonds and pecans 60

porridge, gold top milk, Demerara and roasted plums with bay and vanilla 62

onions: Vulscombe goat's cheese and caramelised red onion tartlets 86

oranges: candy pink rhubarb compote 136

chicken with orange, cream and tarragon 74–5

Christmas glazed ham with clementines and cloves 92–3

dried orange garlands 90–1

meringue roulade with clementine curd, cream and passion fruit 96–8

orange clove pomanders 98

orange, red onion and watercress salad 169

Parmesan: fennel and Parmesan gratin 73

Parmesan and thyme puff pastry twists 46

parsley 34

buttered peas with parsley and chives 42

Cornish crab linguine with chilli, lemon and parsley 104

flat-leaf parsley sauce 95

green sauce for everything, or salsa verde 44

little gem tart with Keen's Cheddar, spring onions and flat-leaf parsley 123

summer carrot salad with flat-leaf parsley and wholegrain dressing 191

passion fruit: meringue roulade with clementine curd, cream and passion fruit 96–8

pasta: Cornish crab linguine with chilli, lemon and parsley 104

weekend spaghetti with garlic and chilli 113

pastries: Cornish pasties 76–7

jammy fig tart topped with crème fraîche and lavender flowers 178

lemon mascarpone tart 80
little gem tart with Keen's
    Cheddar, spring onions
    and flat-leaf parsley 123
Parmesan and thyme puff
    pastry twists 46
peach and almond tart 202–4
tarte tatin with pommes
    230–1
Vulscombe goat's cheese
    and caramelised red onion
    tartlets 86
peach and almond tart 202–4
peas: buttered peas with parsley
    and chives 42
pecans: granola with almonds
    and pecans 60
pistachios: almond and
    pistachio biscotti 142
pistachio nut pudding 63
plums: porridge, gold top milk,
    Demerara and roasted
    plums with bay and vanilla
    62
porridge, gold top milk, Demerara
    and roasted plums with
    bay and vanilla 62
potatoes: roast new potatoes
    with thyme and garlic 42
prawns: English tiger prawns,
    chilli, good olive oil and
    flat-leaf parsley 192
saffron fish stew 220–1
pumpkin: an autumn soup with
    pumpkin, celeriac and
    crispy sage 226

quail's eggs: salad of baby
    artichokes, asparagus,
    leaves and quail eggs with
    lemon dressing and carta
    di musica 117–18
quinces 235
    rich chocolate mousse with
    vanilla ice cream and baked
    quince 233
    the underrated baked quince
    234

rhubarb 137
    candy pink rhubarb compote
    136
    pavlova with whipped cream,
    poached rhubarb and
    pistachios 138
rice: courgette-flower risotto 188

red Camargue rice with feta
    and summer herb salad 166

saffron fish stew 220–1
salads: buffalo mozzarella,
    broad bean, olive, lemon
    and rocket salad 185
cool cucumber salad with
    crème fraîche and dill 161
orange, red onion and
    watercress salad 169
Port Isaac mackerel with a
    raw salad of courgettes,
    chilli, nasturtium flowers
    and rocket 150
red Camargue rice with feta
    and summer herb salad 166
salad of baby artichokes,
    asparagus, leaves and quail
    eggs with lemon dressing
    and carta di musica 117–18
summer carrot salad with
    flat-leaf parsley and
    wholegrain dressing 191
salmon: smoked salmon
    pinwheels 88
    whole baked salmon with
    cucumber, watercress and
    mayonnaise for days 164
salsa verde 44
sandwiches: English cucumber
    sandwiches with salted
    butter 49
sauces: essential, essential
    tomato sauce 44
    flat-leaf parsley sauce 95
    green sauce for everything,
    or salsa verde 44
scallops: hand-dived Cornish
    scallops, pan-fried with
    thyme, garlic and butter
    114
seafood: Cornish crab linguine
    with chilli, lemon and
    parsley 104
    English tiger prawns, chilli,
    good olive oil and flat-leaf
    parsley 192
    hand-dived Cornish scallops,
    pan-fried with thyme,
    garlic and butter 114
    Port Isaac crab, toast and
    mayo 54
    Port Isaac lobster over fire
    with fines herbes 157
    Porthilly mussels, leeks, cider
    and clotted cream 216

saffron fish stew 220–1
skewers: monkfish, Cornish
    chorizo and sun blush
    tomatoes on rosemary
    skewers 158
sole: lemon sole, herb dressing,
    watercress and sea herbs
    64
soup: an autumn soup with
    pumpkin, celeriac and
    crispy sage 226
    Marnie's chicken soup with
    wild garlic, spinach and
    spring herbs 125–6
spinach: Marnie's chicken soup
    with wild garlic, spinach
    and spring herbs 125–6
steak: boeuf bourguignon,
    chestnut mushrooms,
    lardons with winter herbs
    68
strawberries 174
    English strawberries dipped in
    dark chocolate 175
    summer fruit jelly with whole
    English strawberries and
    vanilla ice cream 176
sweets: chocolate and hazelnut
    fudge 36

tarragon 34
    chicken with orange, cream
    and tarragon 74–5
    tarragon mayo 43
toast: Keen's Cheddar on toast
    with sweet leeks 50
    last of the summer tomatoes
    with toasted sourdough
    and high-note herbs 170
    Port Isaac crab, toast and
    mayo 54
    scrambled eggs, wilted wild
    garlic, sourdough toast 109
tomatoes: essential, essential
    tomato sauce 44
    last of the summer tomatoes
    with toasted sourdough
    and high-note herbs 170
    monkfish, Cornish chorizo
    and sun blush tomatoes
    on rosemary skewers 158
tools 31–2

watercress: orange, red onion
    and watercress salad 169
wine 228–9

from
above cove
mill cove
Portland
Sea Campion
Sorrel
dandelion
corn marigold
Chamomile

FORAGE

I search this land
Comb through furze and bramble
Peer into the sward
I enter the greenery
The shrubbery
I forage the foliage

Walking the shoreline
Following the stream and river
Scanning the pool and pond
Sifting the shingle and sediment
Under low skies and high cloud
Foraging in rain and gales, sun and moonshine

To bring home the findings
And trap the game
Snare the essence
Harvest the discoveries
For when I am done with this foraging
My canvas is laden, my paper is complete
Although my appetite is rarely satiated.

LA FIN

LA FIN

Writing this book, I have fallen in love with Cornwall all over again. This is my first book. I never thought I had it in me, and writing it was a wonderful experience that I am so, so happy to have had the opportunity to achieve.

I leave you with the thought of relishing simple pleasures, like sharing toast or sipping coffee together and appreciating everything that this world has to offer. I raise a glass to you and hope to see you in Cornwall one day soon.

Much love, Emily

THANK YOU

To Mark, I love sharing my life with you.

To Oscar, Finn, Evie, Laura, Rosie and Alex, for keeping life real. We are so proud of you and love you.

To my Dadio and mother Luce, for all their support and love, and my talented siblings Harriet, Dan and Fred. Press on, as Grannie Jean would say!

To the strong women in my life.

To Lucius, you always find the right words.

To Papa, for being an inspiration and giving me courage.

To Anthony, thank you for being there for me over the years.

To Kajal, who saw my vision and has brought it to life. I love your creativity and enthusiasm. You are a joy.

To Kim, for bringing my words to life with your beautiful photography.

To Rosie and JoJo, for cooking and being food styling heroes.

To Louie, prop queen.

To Nikki, for the most beautiful of designs.

To you all at Hardie Grant, you are all wonderful; I have loved writing this book with you.

To Heather, for giving me direction in the wonderful world of books.

To you, Team Emily Scott, thank you for your energy, talents, loyalty and commitment. There is never a dull moment.

To Cornwall, my home.

Emily x.

Published in 2021 by Hardie Grant Books, an imprint of Hardie Grant Publishing

Hardie Grant Books (London)
5th & 6th Floors
52–54 Southwark Street
London SE1 1UN

Hardie Grant Books (Melbourne)
Building 1, 658 Church Street
Richmond, Victoria 3121

hardiegrantbooks.com

British Library Cataloguing-in-Publication Data. A catalogue record for this book is available from the British Library.

Sea & Shore ISBN: 978-1-78488-399-7

10 9 8 7 6 5 4 3 2 1

Publisher: Kajal Mistry
Editor: Eila Purvis
Designer: Nikki Ellis
Photographer: Kim Lightbody
Food Stylist: Rosie Ramsden
Prop Stylist: Louie Waller
Photography Assistants: Lesley Lau and Maria Aversa
Food Stylist Assistant: Joanna Jackson
Copy-editor: Emily Preece-Morrison
Proofreader: Susan Low
Indexer: Cathy Heath
Production Controller: Nikolaus Ginelli

Colour reproduction by p2d

Printed and bound in China by Leo Paper Products Ltd.

MIX
Paper from responsible sources
FSC® C020056